PROFILES OF
WOMEN
PAST & PRESENT

PROFILES OF WOMEN

PAST & PRESENT

*Women's History Monologues
for Group Presentations*

VOLUME 2

Created, Researched and Written by Members of the
Thousand Oaks California Branch Inc.
of the American Association of University Women

Illustrated by Ann Mathews

Thousand Oaks California Branch Inc.
American Association of University Women

To order additional copies, send a check for $14.95 each, plus $2.50 shipping and handling (and California sales tax, if applicable) to:

AAUW/Profiles
Thousand Oaks Branch, Inc.
P.O. Box 4223
Thousand Oaks, CA 91359-1223

Please include your name, address, phone number and organization and/ or school district (if applicable) in all correspondence. For information on special discounts on volume orders, write to the above address. Questions and/or comments about your experiences with *Profiles of Women Past & Present* are encouraged and can be sent to the above address.

The fifteen monologues in this book were researched, written, revised and edited by past and/or current members of the Thousand Oaks Branch of the American Association of University Women. We have made our best efforts to verify the accuracy of these histories, within the limitations of conflicting data and scarcity of original sources.

Cover Design: Michelle Webb
Cover Photo: Alan Raphael
Book Design: Deborah Davis

The notable women portrayed on the cover are (bottom row l to r) Yoshiko Uchida by Lily Sugino, Marian Anderson by Fallon Lewis, Julia Morgan by Deana Sun; (top row l to r) Juliette Gordon Low by Alison Diener, Barbara McClintock by Barbara Wilson, Vilma Martinez by Ruth Ann Cooper, Alice Paul by Debbie Trice

First Edition

Library of Congress Catalog Card Number 93-72554

Profiles of women past & present.

Contents Vol. 1: Women's history monologues for group presentations.
Vol. 2: Women's history monologues for group presentations.

1. Monologues. 2. Women-Biography. 3. Drama in education.
I. American Association of University Women. Thousand Oaks California Branch.
II. Title. III. Series
LCPN4305.M6 1996. 812.04508 93-72554

ISBN 0-9637756-1-8

10 9 8 7 6 5 4 3 2 1

Printed in the U.S.A.

This second volume of *Profiles of Women Past & Present* is dedicated to all the individual women and their organizations who are performing these scripts across our country. It is they who are inspiring girls and boys to consider all the possibilities when choosing future careers and encouraging them to overcome real or imagined limitations.

Acknowledgements

We would like to acknowledge the many friends, members and supporters of the Thousand Oaks Branch of the American Association of University Women (AAUW) who helped us shape a dream into a reality:

Lawrence C. Janss and the School of the Pacific Islands who granted funds for publication;

Kate McLean and the Ventura County Community Foundation who facilitated the funding of the grant;

The many members of the Thousand Oaks Branch of AAUW who conceived of the concept, researched, wrote, edited and adapted the monologues and presented these women to schools and groups throughout our community;

The Women's History Publication Committee who compiled, designed, edited, produced and promoted Volume 2 of *Profiles of Women Past & Present*: Joan Bennett, Colleen Briner-Schmidt, Ginny Cobb, Deborah Davis, Pat Helton, Sandy Hindy, Joanne Knapp-Philo, Donna Langley, Jill Lewis, Ann Prehn, Deana Sun, Peggy Tracy, Debbie Trice and Barbara Wilson;

Additionally, Marlene Alexander, Kathy Cresto, Catie Davis, Ronda Eddleman, Wendy Hoffman, Sharon Kaplan, Ricki Mikkelsen, Kathy Myers and Kathleen Sullivan who assisted the committee;

Writers of the monologues: Joan Bennett, Ginny Cobb, Julie Hendrixson, Kathy Hubbard, Therese Hughes, Bev Khoshnevisan, Joanne Knapp-Philo, Donna Langley, Jill Lewis, Janet Madden, Deana Sun, Barbara Wilson and Kerri Yim;

The many people who reviewed the scripts and offered their expert advice in order to make the scripts as accurate as possible: Opal M. Anderson of the Susan LaFlesche Picotte Center, Maya Angelou, Judith Baca, Tanya Bresinsky of the Maria Mitchell Association, Nathaniel Comfort of the Cold Spring Harbor Laboratory (Barbara McClintock), John Horn of the California Department of Parks and Recreation (Julia Morgan), Barbara Irvine of the Alice Paul Foundation, Katherine Keena of the Juliette Gordon Low Girl Scout National Center, Wilma Mankiller, Vilma Martinez and Gerald D. Yoshitomi of the Japanese American Cultural and Community Center (Yoshiko Uchida);

And finally, the girls and boys in the classrooms who have applauded our presentations and encouraged us in our endeavors.

Table of Contents

Introduction and History

How many students know that . . . Vilma Martinez was a founder of the Mexican American Legal Defense and Educational Fund (MALDEF), an organization that works to fight discrimination against Mexican Americans? . . . Alice Paul went to jail because she believed women should have the right to vote? . . . Dr. Susan LaFlesche Picotte was the first Native American woman to become a medical doctor? . . . Wilma Rudolph overcame polio to become the first woman to win three gold medals in one Olympics?

Very few, according to Dr. David and the late Dr. Myra Sadker, authors of *Failing at Fairness: How America's Schools Cheat Girls*, and professors of education at the American University in Washington, D.C. In fact, when the Sadkers challenged high school students to name twenty famous U.S. women from the past OR present, most of them were able to name only four or five. The reason? Because few pages—even in brand new history books—focus on the lives or accomplishments of women. The Sadkers' research indicated that acquainting girls with women of achievement opens up the possibilities for future careers, inspires higher achievement and increases their self-esteem.

In March of 1987, members of the Thousand Oaks Branch of the American Association of University Women (AAUW) created a Women's History Project, an innovative way to introduce students to the lives and accomplishments of women like those mentioned above. Every year during Women's History Month in March, hundreds of women and young girls in the community rehearse monologues researched and written by members of the Thousand Oaks Branch of AAUW, create authentic costumes and visit classrooms to portray five notable women from history.

These classroom "visits" have been popular with local students, teachers, principals and parents over the years. Consequently, Volume 1 of *Profiles of Women Past & Present* was published in 1993. This book contained fifteen of the original first-person monologues researched and written for classroom presentations. The Thousand Oaks Branch of AAUW is proud to present fifteen new monologues in Volume 2, along with the suggested costumes, props and presentation ideas. It is hoped this second volume will continue to inspire women and girls across the country to visit classrooms and make women's history "come alive" for students in their own communities.

Getting Started

The living history approach in this book brings history to life for elementary and intermediate students. It is particularly appropriate for these grades because it provides a multisensory experience, allowing students to actively see, hear, respond and question. It is also an appropriate way to introduce multicultural role models into the history/social science curriculum.

The monologues can be used in a variety of ways. They can be simplified or adapted beyond the two versions provided here, as required for particular audiences. You are encouraged to use your imagination and be as creative as possible in their use.

Teachers, community volunteers or students dressed in costume can present the monologues to small groups, individual classrooms or school assemblies. The monologues can be memorized or read aloud. One woman can be presented each day for one week or several women can be presented at one time.

It is important to obtain prior approval from the superintendent, board of education and/or school principals in your area. The following samples are provided for your convenience in this book and may be easily revised to meet your particular needs:

> Sample letters to school districts, school principals and
> classroom presenters
> Sample media release and radio/television spots

Also in this book are two items for distribution to teachers:
> Sample announcement flyer
> Suggested classroom activities

For each monologue, the following items are provided:
> A full-page illustration
> Suggestions for costume and props
> Notes/tips for presenters
> Suggested reading

There are numerous rewards for presenters. Months after the presentations, children often meet the presenters in the community and exclaim, "I know you! You're Annie Smith Peck," or "Aren't you Julia Morgan? I want to be an architect when I grow up." It is extremely gratifying to help students realize there are no limits to the goals they set or the careers they choose.

General Suggestions for Presenters

Being a presenter is a gratifying experience. For a short time, you can be that famous woman you read about as a school girl or only recently discovered as an adult. To aid you in preparing for your performances, the following general suggestions were gathered from past presenters. Specific characteristics unique to each woman are listed after each monologue. You are encouraged to use your imagination and ingenuity to make your presentation a memorable experience for both you and your audience.

Promoting Interest

Talk to the school librarian in advance about doing a Women's History Month bulletin board in the library and setting out books about the women who will be portrayed, as well as other notable women.

The school cafeteria is another good location for a Women's History Month bulletin board to promote discussion among the students. If time allows, change the board daily to highlight the woman of the day. Add news articles, photographs, copies of written material, etc.

Finding Costumes and Props

Costume shops can provide great ideas for costumes, but the best places to find materials for costumes and props are thrift shops. They are also less expensive. By asking other presenters, friends, neighbors and relatives for help in acquiring items, you will incur little or no expense.

Don't be afraid to enhance your costume, to be dramatic and to stand out. You are there to make an impression and you definitely will. The students will remember you for years to come.

If you are portraying a person of another race, be sure to explain your character's ethnicity during the presentation. Many of our notable women represent varying races and cultures. Visual aids such as photographs, clothing and hairstyle will enhance the image. We suggest you exhibit good taste and sensitivity. Ask the children to use their imaginations.

Rehearsing the Monologue

It is not really necessary to memorize the monologue. It is a good idea to know it very well so you can tell it in your own words, but there is nothing wrong with reading it aloud. Most of the presenters carry props that afford good hiding places for a condensed monologue or outline.

Knowing Your Character

Keep in mind these monologues are very condensed versions of one person's entire lifetime. The monologues may need to be updated with regard to the woman's present status. Doing a little studying on your own prior to the presentation will give you a better insight into the person you are portraying and may provide answers to questions the students might ask. The better you know your part, the easier this is.

Scheduling Your Time

Respect the classroom time you have been allotted and answer limited questions. If the teacher is open to your staying longer, take into consideration your own time schedule for presentations in other classrooms. If time is limited, or if you do not feel comfortable answering questions, refer the students to the library and suggest they find the answers and even more information.

Portraying Your Character

If possible ask the teacher to welcome you and explain the purpose of your visit when you arrive. Keep in mind that it is important for you to stay in character throughout your presentation. When answering a student's question, respond in the first person.

Having Confidence

Keep in mind the children will be fascinated and appreciative of what you are doing. It does not occur to them that you may be feeling shy or nervous about standing in front of them. They will BELIEVE in you and the woman you are presenting.

MARIAN ANDERSON

MARIAN ANDERSON (1902–1993)

I was the first black person to sing at the Metropolitan Opera in New York City.

Do you think that people with great talent grow up and become famous just because they are good at soccer or music? Well, as I found out, it takes a lot of study and practice. I had a beautiful voice, so I became a concert singer. The famous conductor Arturo Toscanini said, "A voice like hers is heard once in a hundred years." My name is Marian Anderson.

I was born in Philadelphia in 1902. At that time, black people were not allowed the same privileges as white people. I first sang in our Union Baptist Church choir when I was 6, and sometimes we traveled on trains to sing in churches in other cities. In Southern states we could not stay in a hotel or eat in some restaurants because of our dark skin. Once, after a concert, I was presented the key to the city, but I was not allowed to stay there.

When I was small, my two sisters and I had many happy times, like going to the circus and taking vacations on trains. But my father died when I was 10 and my mother had to get a job. We didn't have enough money to pay for singing lessons, but people in our community raised money to pay for mine. I worked hard and became skilled enough to enter a singing contest. The prize was a chance to sing with the New York Philharmonic Orchestra. Well, I entered and I won. How exciting it was to go to New York City to sing in a big concert hall!

At 21, I went on a concert tour of European countries. The people there liked me very much and did not seem to care about my dark skin. Instead, they made me feel welcome. I learned the songs that European people liked to hear and I brought American music to them. One of the hardest things I had to learn was to sing in three other languages: Italian, Spanish and German.

In the United States, prejudice still existed against black people. In Washington, D.C., I was not allowed to sing in Constitution Hall because I was black. That made many people angry. So on Easter Sunday of 1939, it was arranged for me to sing outdoors in

CONCERT SINGER

front of the Lincoln Memorial. Over 75,000 people came to hear me. I felt greatly honored to sing at Abraham Lincoln's Memorial because he had done so much to help black people when he was President.

I continued to sing in cities around the world and my concerts were always packed. I was the first black person to sing at the Metropolitan Opera in New York City. After 1955, I could stay in hotels wherever I wished, but it bothered me that other black people were not treated as fairly. Just as people had once helped me, I finally had enough money to help many young singers pay for their music lessons.

Because of my successful singing career and because I cared so much about equality for all people, I became one of the most admired women in the world. In 1957, President Eisenhower asked me to sing "The Star-Spangled Banner" at his inauguration. It was a great honor. Soon the United States government sent me on goodwill tours to other countries and named me a United States delegate to the United Nations. I went to Asia, Africa and what was then called the Soviet Union and was greeted by heads of state everywhere.

When I was 62 years old, I retired from singing. My husband and I went to live at our home in the country, which we called Marianna Farm.

On my 75th birthday in 1977, President Jimmy Carter presented me with a special Congressional Medal for devotion to the promotion of the arts. I was also awarded the United Nations Peace Prize. I lived to be 91 years old, proud of my contributions to music and worldwide peace and understanding. The citation on the Presidential Medal of Freedom which I received in 1963 reads, "Marian Anderson has ennobled her race and her country, while her voice has enthralled the world."

COSTUME/PROPS

Long evening dress (white or blue)

Sheet music

Pictures of Lincoln Memorial, Metropolitan Opera

NOTES/TIPS FOR PRESENTERS:

Stand near a piano.

Let students see notes on sheet music.

Define "prejudice" and "pre-judge" by writing on board.

Explain "goodwill tours" and "heads of state."

Explain what a "key to the city" means.

Show Philadelphia, Washington, D.C. and New York City on a map.

Play a recording of Anderson's music in the background.

SUGGESTED READING:

Altman, Susan. *Extraordinary Black Americans From Colonial to Contemporary Times*. Chicago: Children's Press, 1989.

Anderson, Marian. *My Lord What a Morning*. New York: Viking Press, 1956.

McKissack, Patricia and Frederick McKissack. *Marian Anderson: A Great Singer*. Hillside, N.J.: Enslow Publishers, 1991.

Patterson, Charles. *Marian Anderson*. New York: Watts, 1988.

Stevenson, Janet. *Marian Anderson: Singing for the World*. Chicago: Encyclopaedia Britannica Press, 1963.

Tedards, Anne. *Marian Anderson*. New York: Chelsea House, 1988.

Vehanen, Kosti. *Marian Anderson, A Portrait*. McGraw, 1941.

MAYA
ANGELOU

MAYA ANGELOU
(1928–   )

I have written many

poems, plays, songs

and books about

my life.

My name is Maya Angelou (AN-jel-oh). I was born in 1928 in St. Louis, Missouri. When I was 3 years old and my brother Bailey was 4, our parents got a divorce and sent us to live with our grandmother. We were put on a train by ourselves with a tag attached to our wrists that said:

> "To Whom It May Concern: This is Marguerite and Bailey Johnson, Jr. from Long Beach, California, en route to Stamps, Arkansas, c/o Mrs. Annie Henderson."

In those days, we were not allowed to do the same things as white people. We went to different schools and never went into the neighborhoods where white people lived. One time when I had an infected tooth, my grandmother took me to the white dentist. Even though I was really sick, he told her that he would not take care of a Negro. We had to ride a bus to another town to find a dentist to help me.

Our grandmother taught Bailey and me to work hard and to trust in God. Bailey was my best friend. He gave me the name Maya because when he was little he used to call me "mine" and it sounded like Maya.

When I was a teenager, I moved to San Francisco to live with my mother. While in high school, I studied dance and drama. But mostly, I felt lonely and when I was 16, I got pregnant without realizing what I was getting into. My son, Guy, was born three weeks after I graduated from high school and I had to find a way to support the two of us.

Over the next several years, I had many jobs. I was everything from a cook to a night club dancer and singer. I also became the first black woman conductor on the San Francisco streetcars. Once I met a man who was really nice to me and whom I trusted. But when he offered me drugs, I was lucky enough to realize that if I got involved with drugs, I would not be able to take care of my son, so I moved away.

POET, WRITER

I was also very lucky when I was offered a part in *Porgy and Bess*. This musical was unusual for the time because it was about black people and their lives. We traveled to 22 nations for performances. I was able to meet many different people and to learn several languages.

In the 1960s I joined the Civil Rights Movement and worked with the Reverend Dr. Martin Luther King Jr. I was very honored when he asked me to become the Northern Coordinator of the Southern Christian Leadership Conference. During that time, I wrote a play with Godfrey Cambridge called *Cabaret for Freedom* to raise money for our cause.

When my son Guy was a teenager, I married a man who was a South African freedom fighter. We moved to the continent of Africa, where we lived in Egypt and Ghana. We realized it was the "first time in our lives when the color of our skin was accepted as correct and normal." I worked as an assistant administrator of a university, and a writer and editor for print media and television. This was unusual because women in Africa are not usually allowed to work at jobs outside their homes.

Since that time, I have written many poems, plays, songs and books about my life. *I Know Why The Caged Bird Sings* is the story of my childhood and has been made into a movie. My film, *Georgia, Georgia*, was the first movie ever written by an African American woman.

My life has been filled with many honors. I have been honored by Presidents Ford, Carter and Bush. In 1992, President-elect Clinton asked me to write a poem to read at his inauguration. I am a director, a lecturer and a teacher, and I am currently the Reynolds professor for American Studies at Wake Forest University in North Carolina. This is a lifetime appointment.

I live by the rule that my mother and grandmother taught me when I was small: "You may encounter many defeats, but you must not be defeated."

COSTUME/PROPS

African design print skirt or dress in bright colors

A head wrap to accompany outfit

Large, dramatic African jewelry

NOTES/TIPS FOR PRESENTERS:

Angelou is six feet tall and moves with the fluid grace of a dancer. She exudes the confidence of her internal strength. She uses her hands, posture and commanding voice to inspire her audience.

Read Angelou's poem from President Clinton's inauguration, "On the Pulse of Morning."

Students may write to Angelou at 2720 Reynolds Road, #9, Winston-Salem, NC 27106.

SUGGESTED READING:

Angelou, Maya. *I Know Why the Caged Bird Sings*. New York: Random House, 1970.

Angelou, Maya. *Gather Together In My Name*. New York: Random House, 1974.

Angelou, Maya. *Oh Pray My Wings Are Gonna Fit Me Well*. New York: Random House, 1975.

Angelou, Maya. *Singin' and Swingin' and Gettin' Merry Like Christmas*. New York: Random House, 1976.

Angelou, Maya. *And Still I Rise*. New York: Random House, 1978.

Angelou, Maya. *The Heart of a Woman*. New York: Random House, 1981.

Angelou, Maya. *Shaker, Why don't You Sing?* New York: Random House, 1983.

Angelou, Maya. *All God's Children Need Traveling Shoes*. New York: Vintage Books, 1986.

Angelou, Maya. *On the Pulse of Morning*. New York: Random House, 1993.

King, Sarah E. *Maya Angelou: Greeting the Morning*. Brookfield, CT.: Millbrook Press, 1994.

Shapiro, Miles. *Maya Angelou*. New York: Chelsea House, 1994.

Terry, Gayle Pollard. "Maya Angelou: Creating a Poem to Honor the Nation." *Los Angeles Times*, January 17, 1993.

Judith Baca

JUDITH BACA
(1946–   )

I helped develop over

250 murals that were

painted around Los

Angeles by young

people of all colors

and backgrounds.

Mi abuela, my grandmother, believed people who hurt others had been badly hurt themselves. Sometimes, people would stare at her because she looked like an Apache Indian with her long dark braids. But she was not an Apache; she was from Mexico. Once a store owner tried to cheat her, thinking she would not understand because she spoke only *español*. My grandmother asked me to tell him in *inglés* that he had given her the incorrect change. He was rude, but my grandmother returned his hatred with kindness because she knew he had a hard life and probably had been treated wrongly before by someone else. She taught me to treat everybody *con respecto*, with respect.

Me llamo, my name, is Judith Baca and I am an artist and activist. That means I believe taking art to people *es muy importante*, is very important, and can change how people think about others. I was born in Watts, California in 1946 and am a Chicana, which means that *mi familia*, my family, came from the country of Mexico. I paint murals and help others organize mural painting in their neighborhoods. A mural is a large picture painted right on a wall.

I started to paint when I was in elementary school. Because I spoke English poorly, my kindergarten *maestra*, teacher, would let me sit in a corner and paint. Once I started painting, I found a way to express myself without words. At home there was no extra *dinero*, money, to buy paints but *mi madre*, my mother, proudly displayed all my art.

I graduated from college with a degree in art in 1969. I found a job with the City of Los Angeles and taught art at parks and *escuelas*, schools. During lunch time, I would watch the kids who hung out at the park and I began to notice they expressed themselves with their tattoos, special clothing and graffiti. I decided to form a group of *muchachos*, boys and girls, ages 14 to 20 called *Las Vistas Nuevas*, which means New Views. *Juntos pintamos*, together we painted, a mural *en una pared*, on a wall, at a local park. The kids were from different gangs and neighborhoods but had found a way to work together.

MURAL ARTIST

Next, I studied the great Mexican muralists and eventually went to Mexico for lessons in mural painting. *Cuando volví a mi casa*, when I returned home, I expanded my art program into the "Citywide Mural Project." I helped develop over 250 murals that were painted around Los Angeles by young people of all colors and backgrounds.

In 1976, I had an idea for a project titled "The Great Wall of Los Angeles," a mural painted on the Tujunga Wash in the San Fernando Valley. It is a half-mile long and took *nueve años*, nine years, to complete. It shows pictures of the City of Los Angeles and its many peoples and history. I hired the muralists, mostly young people, *de todos colores*, of all colors, and raised the money. It was so rewarding for everyone that I started the Social and Public Art Resource Center, called SPARC. It is now a public art center known worldwide.

In 1987, I developed an idea for a mural called "The World Wall: A Vision of the Future Without Fear." It is a movable mural about peace and cooperation. It occurred to me that for many people it was easier to imagine destruction than to imagine peace. One of my *estudiantes*, students, wondered if we all share the same idea of peace. He asked me, "Is peace everyone sitting around watching TV?" If we cannot imagine what peace is, how can we ever hope for it to happen?

I believe artists *tienen el poder*, have the power, to spread ideas and the responsibility to dream. The "World Wall" is one way ideas about peace can travel around the world. As the mural goes to other countries, each nation's artists add their vision of a world without fear.

Today, I am a *profesora* of art at the University of California at Irvine where I teach classes on murals and public art. One of my latest projects is called "Cultural Explainers." Doorways and bridges will be turned into monuments to show and share the different cultures of our city. It will be like a big "show and tell" explaining why people are different and what makes them the same. *Como mi abuela*, like my grandmother, taught me when I was a little girl, when we learn to accept others, we stop spreading hate and start spreading peace.

COSTUME/PROPS

Jeans and T-shirt or a simple dress

Colored photocopies of Baca's murals

Painter's palette

NOTES/TIPS FOR PRESENTERS:

Ask students how many of them have seen or made a mural.

Ask if they like to paint.

Have them make a class mural.

Ask students what they think the world would be like without fear.

Ask students to explain what culture is. What is their culture?

Suggest reading about other muralists (Rivera, Siqueiros, Orozco).

A biography, resume and press articles on Baca are available from Social and Public Art Resource Center (SPARC), Venice, CA. Phone: (310) 922-9560.

SUGGESTED READING:

Estrada, Anne. "Judy Baca's Art for Peace." *Hispanic*, May, 1991, 16–18.

SPANISH PRONUNCIATION GUIDE

como mi abuela	COH-moh mee ah-BWEH-lah
con respecto	cohn ray-SPECK-toh
cuando volví a mi casa	CWAHN-doh vohl-VEE ah mee CAH-sah
de todos colores	day TOH-dohs coh-LOH-res
dinero	dee-NAY-roh
en una pared	en OO-nah pah-RED
es muy importante	es mwee im-pohr-TAHN-tay
escuelas	es-CWAY-lahs
español	es-pahn-YOHL
estudiantes	es-too-dee-AHN-tes
inglés	eeng-LESS
juntos pintamos	HOON-tohs peen-TAH-mohs
las vistas nuevas	lahs VEES-tahs NWAY-vahs
maestra	mah-ES-trah
me llamo	may YAH-moh
mi madre	mee MAH-dray
mi familia	mee fah-MEEL-yah
mi abuela	mee a-BWEH-lah
muchachos	moo-CHAH-chos
nueve años	NWEH-vay AHN-yohs
profesora	proh-feh-SOH-rah
tienen el poder	TYEH-nen el poh-DEHR

SUSAN BUTCHER

SUSAN BUTCHER
(1954–)

Can you imagine living in a log cabin in Alaska and taking care of 150 dogs every day? Well, if you can, you'd be imagining my life. I really do have 150 dogs, mostly Siberian and Alaskan Huskies, and I raise them for dogsled racing. I'm famous in Alaska and around the world because I have won the Iditarod International Sled Dog Race four times. I'm Susan Butcher.

I haven't always lived in Alaska. I was born in 1954 in Massachusetts. Even when I was young, I didn't like city living. I wanted my parents to tear down our house and build a tiny log cabin so there would be more room for grass and trees.

School was often hard for me because I had dyslexia. When I saw the word *now* (n-o-w), I might read it as *won* (w-o-n). My teachers often told me I was lazy or not applying myself when I had trouble understanding something I had read. I did much better in sports, and I competed in softball, basketball, field hockey, running and swimming.

After I graduated from high school, I moved to Colorado and worked as a veterinarian's assistant. I met a woman who trained dogs for dogsled racing, or "mushing," as we call it in Alaska. One day in 1973, I read about the very first Iditarod Sled Dog Race. The Iditarod was being started so people would remember how important dogsledding had been in Alaska's history. The race would be over 1,000 miles long and follow the same trail used by mushers almost one hundred years ago to transport mail, supplies and gold. The trail would cross over icy tundra, frozen rivers, dense forests and rugged mountains. I knew right away that I would race in the Iditarod someday.

Two years later, I moved to Alaska. I bought several dogs and started working on my dog training and mushing skills. I lived in a small cabin in the Alaskan bush. The only way to reach my cabin was by plane! I chopped firewood, hauled water from a creek and hunted for food. I woke up at 5:30 every morning to feed my

IDITAROD CHAMPION

dogs before taking them on practice runs of twenty to sixty miles. Afterward, I would rub the dogs' sore muscles. I treated my dogs with respect and affection. I learned to trust their instincts about the wilderness and they learned they could depend on me. My dogs became my family and my friends.

I entered the Iditarod for the first time in 1978, and finished 19th. During the next six years, I always finished in the top ten. In 1985, I was racing my best team ever when suddenly my team and I came upon a moose blocking the trail. The moose charged and began attacking my dogs. I grabbed my ax and went after the moose. After about twenty minutes, another musher came along the trail and shot the moose. Two of my dogs died and several others were badly injured, so I had to drop out of the race. Libby Riddles won that year, crushing my hopes of being the first woman to win the Iditarod.

After so many years of trying to win and experiencing the moose attack, you might think I would not want to race again. But I did, and the next year, in 1986, I won the Iditarod in record-breaking time! I won again in 1987 and 1988, becoming the first person to win three Iditarod races in a row. I won again in 1990.

I love everything about the Iditarod: the mountain views, the wild animals and the lonely trails. It's not just competing against other dogs and drivers, but against unpredictable forces in nature and my own fatigue, cold and sleeplessness. I'm really happy when I'm out on the trail mushing, or caring for my dogs. "The Iditarod is something that was made for me."

COSTUME/PROPS

Parka with a fur-lined hood and a racing number over parka

Stocking cap, heavy gloves and boots

Iditarod equipment (sleeping bag, camp stove, first aid kit, dog food)

Picture of dog team and sled

With prior approval, you might want to take an Alaskan Husky or similar breed with you

NOTES/TIPS FOR PRESENTERS:

Iditarod is derived from *"Haiditarod,"* an Indian word that means a distant place. Mush is derived from *"marche,"* a French word that means march.

Call Iditarod at 800-545-6874 for a free catalog of maps, Iditarod patches and T-shirts that might be useful.

Have students plot the Iditarod Trail on a map of Alaska.

Look for articles and/or TV coverage about the Iditarod, which starts the first weekend of March.

Introduce *Mush!* by Patricia Seibert or *Black Star, Bright Dawn* by Scott O'Dell for the students to read.

Watch the film *Iron Will.*

SUGGESTED READING:

Coman, Carolyn. *Body & Soul: Ten American Women.* Boston: Hill & Co., Publishers, 1988.

"Musher." *The New Yorker*, October 5, 1987.

Mueller, Larry. "Arctic Adventures." *Outdoor Life*, January, 1991.

Sherwonit, Bill. *Iditarod: The Great Race to Nome.* Anchorage: Northwest Books, 1991.

Steptoe, Sonja. "The Dogged Pursuit of Excellence." *Sports Illustrated*, February 11, 1991.

JULIETTE GORDON LOW

Juliette Gordon Low (1860–1927)

In 1913, I founded

the Girl Scouts of

the U.S.A.

When I was a child, my favorite game was to act out the stories my Grandmother Kinzie told us about her adventures in the wilderness. I never tired of that world of make-believe and adventure and, when I grew up, I kept that world open for many girls and their grown-up leaders.

My name is Juliette Magill Kinzie Gordon Low and I founded the Girl Scouts of the U.S.A. I was named after my pioneer grandmother, but my family called me Daisy. I was born in Savannah, Georgia, just before the Civil War began.

I was an independent and outspoken child. My sister Nellie called me "Crazy Daisy" because I was so unpredictable. I enjoyed making up games, writing and acting in plays, and playing with my pet animals.

When I turned 13, my parents sent me to boarding school in Virginia where I studied English, history and literature. Three years later I went to a finishing school in New York City. The school was so strict that we were required to speak only French and were seldom allowed outside the building except in the company of our teachers. I was very talented at painting and drawing, but a poor student in spelling and math.

After I finished my schooling I traveled extensively, including two trips to Europe where I met William Low, a wealthy businessman. We were married in Georgia and left on our honeymoon, but had to return two days later because a piece of wedding rice had become lodged in my ear. When the doctor tried to remove it, I became totally deaf in that ear. An ear infection had earlier left me partially deaf in my other ear, so I had very limited hearing. But I was not the kind of person to be stopped by a handicap.

Once we settled in England, we lived very well. We traveled all over the world, socializing with nobility and celebrities.

When my husband died in 1905, he left a very confusing will, so for several years I had to worry about money, something I had never done before. My poor math skills made matters worse

FOUNDER OF GIRL SCOUTS OF THE U.S.A.

because I was never sure how much money I had. But I continued to travel and still gave away money to people in need.

I finally returned to London where I met Sir Robert Baden-Powell. He told me about his work with the Boy Scouts and also about the Girl Guide program he started. I was so impressed that within weeks I had started a Girl Guide company. Later, I returned to America to start Girl Guiding there. I had found a purpose in my life and was the happiest I had ever been. I gave the girls of Savannah the opportunity to play basketball, take nature hikes, go camping and learn about boys and girls in other lands. Some parents were shocked because they expected more ladylike activities, but most assumed anything I endorsed was acceptable.

In fact, there was so much interest in scouting, I decided to set up a national organization. In 1913, I founded the Girl Scouts of the U.S.A., with headquarters in Washington, D.C. I was convinced Girl Scouting and Girl Guiding could make the world a better place. While World War I raged, Girl Scouts across the nation participated in Red Cross work, sold Liberty Bonds and worked as nurses. The First Lady, Mrs. Woodrow Wilson, invited me to the White House and praised the work of the Girl Scouts. Girl Scouting had finally received the national acceptance and recognition it deserved.

I believed so strongly in Girl Scouting that for years I paid all the expenses, using money obtained through fund-raising. But I had built a strong organization. I helped start regional camps for girls and training of their leaders, designed an official uniform, wrote a guide book and established a national headquarters. In 1926, I succeeded in bringing girls from other countries to the United States for the World Camp. I wanted campers and leaders from around the world to think of each other as friends and neighbors.

I died in 1927 and was buried in my full uniform, with a tin cup and knife at my belt. In my pocket was a telegram from Girl Scout Headquarters that read, "You are not only the first Girl Scout, but the best Girl Scout of them all."

COSTUME/PROPS

Girl Scout uniform/hat

Girl Scout guide book

Enlarged copy of Girl Scout logo

Nature books

Hiking equipment (stick, compass, tin cup, knife, boots, canteen)

NOTES/TIPS TO PRESENTERS:

Define a "finishing school."

Explain "First Lady."

Point out England and Georgia on a map.

Juliette Low had a very pronounced British accent when she returned from Great Britain.

SUGGESTED READING:

Behrens, June. *Juliette Low: Founder of the Girl Scouts of America*. Chicago: Children's Press, 1988.

Kudlinski, Kathleen V. *Juliette Gordon Low: America's First Girl Scout*. New York: Viking Kestrel, 1988.

Peavy, Linda S. and Ursula Smith. *Dreams into Deeds: Nine Women Who Dared*. New York: Charles Scribners Sons, 1985.

Steelsmith, Shari. *Juliette Gordon Low: Founder of the Girl Scouts*. Seattle: Parenting Press, 1990.

Worlds To Explore: Handbook for Brownie and Junior Girl Scouts. New York: Girl Scouts of the U.S.A., 1984.

WILMA MANKILLER

WILMA MANKILLER
(1945–   )

From 1985 to 1994 I was

the Principal Chief of the

Cherokee Nation, the

second largest Native

American tribe.

Among the Cherokee, names are important. My family name, Asgaya-dihi, was the word for a military leader who demonstrated strength and courage. In English, it means "mankiller." I am Wilma Pearl Mankiller and from 1985 to 1994 I was the Principal Chief of the Cherokee Nation, the second largest Native American tribe. My job as chief was like that of all leaders: to help the Cherokee people take care of themselves and their families, be healthy, have jobs and be safe.

Every Cherokee is a part of the past, the present and the future, and my family has been important throughout my life. My father was a full-blooded Cherokee and my mother, Dutch and Irish. I have six brothers and four sisters. I was born on November 18, 1945 in Oklahoma.

The Cherokee people have not always lived in Oklahoma. Before the white men came to America, we lived in the Southeast. In 1838 the government decided our land was needed for white people and that the Cherokees needed to be "relocated." The Cherokee people were rounded up, held in corrals like cattle and forced to walk all the way from North Carolina to Oklahoma. Thousands of Cherokee people died and this event has become known as the Trail of Tears.

My family had a "trail of tears" of its own. When I was 12, we moved to San Francisco. There had been a two-year drought and our farm was not able to produce enough to support us. The only help the government would give was to "relocate" us to a city. They believed that Indians would become more like other Americans if they lived away from other Indians. When we got to San Francisco, my family and I were shocked! We had never had indoor toilets or electricity. We were used to night sounds of crickets, coyotes and owls, so we were frightened by the city sounds of sirens, breaking glass, shouting and fighting. Our hotel had a box that opened up in the wall. People got into it, it closed up and they disappeared! My brothers and sisters and I walked up the stairs instead of using the elevator so we would not disappear too!

CHIEF OF THE CHEROKEE NATION

I did not feel I belonged in the city. My sister and I practiced every night so we would sound like the other kids in our school, but it did not help. We were still different. After many years, we finally got used to San Francisco. I graduated from high school, got married and had two daughters.

In 1969, a group of Native Americans took over Alcatraz, an old federal prison located on an island in San Francisco Bay. They were protesting the way Indians were treated. I worked to support them and realized I needed to return to our land to help the Cherokee people. My daughters and I moved to Mankiller Flats and I built a new house near my childhood home. I went to college and worked to improve living conditions in our area. One significant change took place after the people of Bell, Oklahoma, worked to get 16 miles of water pipe laid; for the first time, they had running water in their homes.

Life has always presented hardships to the Cherokee people, and I have had my share. I was in a car accident and it took seventeen operations to enable me to walk again. Then they discovered I had a disease similar to muscular dystrophy. I still take medicine for this. Finally, I needed a kidney transplant. As always, my family helped. My brother gave me one of his kidneys.

At the time I was elected chief, many people thought the Cherokee would not want a woman to be chief. Actually, before the white people came, Cherokee women were as important as men in our culture. I believe I have followed in the footsteps of Cherokee women before me and that my people are more concerned about jobs and education than about whether or not the tribe is run by a woman.

Although I am no longer chief, I continue my work. We are a modern people who need to hold on to the best of our past: our language, our ceremonies and our culture. That is the challenge of the future for all Native Americans and I am one part of that struggle.

COSTUME/PROPS

Contemporary business suit

U.S. map showing Trail of Tears

NOTES/TIPS FOR PRESENTERS:

The terms "Indian" and "Native American" used in this monologue are consistent with their usage over Mankiller's lifetime.

Mankiller's spirituality is said to permeate her presence. As the script indicates, her predominant value is not her individual accomplishments, but rather her contribution to the continuum of life that is the Cherokee people. In portraying this woman, stereotypical "Indian costumes" should not be used.

Trace the Trail of Tears on a map from North Carolina to Oklahoma.

Ask students to imagine what it would be like not to have electricity or running water in their houses.

Explain "drought" and its effect on farming.

Refer to the Removal Act in U.S. history.

Explain Alcatraz and the protest.

Students may write to Mankiller through her publisher:
St. Martin's Press, 175 Fifth Avenue, New York, New York.

SUGGESTED READING:

Mankiller, W.P. and Michael Wallis. *Mankiller: A Chief and Her People*. New York: St. Martin's Press, 1994.

Rand, J.T. *Wilma Mankiller*. Austin, Texas: Raintree Steck-Vaughn, 1993.

Simon, C. *Wilma P. Mankiller: Chief of the Cherokee*. Chicago: Children's Press, 1991.

Wallace, M. "Wilma Mankiller." *Ms.*, January, 1988.

Vilma Martinez

MALDEF

VILMA MARTINEZ
(1943–   )

Hello. I'm Vilma Martinez. I'm an attorney and I work for a law firm in Los Angeles. I handle cases between big companies and workers who feel they have been treated unfairly. Can everyone hear me? I know I speak softly; as a matter of fact, I never shout. I believe WHAT you say is more important than how loudly you say it.

I grew up in a poor neighborhood of San Antonio, Texas. My father was from Mexico and my mother was from Texas. I was the oldest of five children. One day, we were very excited because our church group was going on a picnic. At the last minute, it was canceled because Mexican Americans were not allowed to use the park. Can you imagine how we felt? We were hurt and angry.

But I knew being hurt and angry wouldn't make things better. I would have to DO something. At school, I learned to speak English, and I read a lot and studied hard. I got straight A's in every class.

I went to the University of Texas. Most people take four years to graduate from college, but I did it in two and a half. I was in a hurry because I was afraid I would not have enough money to finish.

For a while, I worked with a lawyer in San Antonio. I liked the way he was able to help people. I decided to go to Columbia Law School in New York City. When I went to interview for a scholarship to help me pay for my classes, the man asked, "Why should we give you a scholarship? You are a woman, and you are going to be married and have children. You are not going to practice law. We will be wasting our investment." I told him I hadn't been working SO long and SO hard not to practice law. I got the scholarship.

I graduated when I was 24. I met my future husband, Stuart Singer, while we were both studying for law exams. Stuart was the only man I ever met who said, "Vilma, you're not tough enough." And that's just what I was waiting to hear.

CIVIL RIGHTS LEADER

I began working as a lawyer in New York defending workers' rights and gaining valuable experience. It was nice not to hear what I had heard all through school: "You are so bright—for a Mexican." Instead, I was being accepted for my ability as a lawyer.

In 1968, the Mexican American Legal Defense and Educational Fund, or MALDEF, was started. Later on, when they needed someone to be in charge, I became the head of MALDEF.

One of our early struggles had to do with the right to vote. At election time in certain states, Mexican Americans were discouraged from voting or even registering to vote. Through MALDEF's efforts, Mexican American citizens are now assured the right to vote and, in areas where many of them do not speak English, the ballots are printed in English and Spanish.

Another important victory was for the children in public schools who do not speak English. We fought for and won their right to be taught in both English and Spanish.

In 1981, I decided to leave MALDEF. I was proud of its accomplishments and felt I was leaving it in good shape. I considered running for public office or teaching college. I finally decided to join the law firm I am with today. It was a refreshing change to return to the pure joys of law practice and I liked having more time to spend with my sons, Carlos and Ricardo.

I believe all students should be able to finish school knowing that if they work hard and do well, they will be rewarded. In 1993, my name appeared on lists for President Clinton to consider when he was choosing a new justice for the Supreme Court.

I have been lucky to participate in one of the most important and challenging eras for Mexican American citizens in this country. We have made great progress, but there is still much to be done so our country can deliver on its promise of equal opportunity for all its people.

COSTUME/PROPS

Skirted suit—purple or dark rose

Soft-sided briefcase

NOTES/TIPS FOR PRESENTERS:

Point to San Antonio, New York, Los Angeles on U.S. map.

Write MALDEF on board.

Students may write to Martinez at Munger, Tolles and Olson, 355 S. Grand Avenue, 35th Floor, Los Angeles, CA 90071.

SUGGESTED READING:

"A Quiet but Effective Fighter for Mexican American Rights." *New York Times*, May 19, 1978, A14.

Benevidez, Max. "Vilma Martinez: Pulling No Punches." *Equal Opportunity Forum*, March, 1982, 22-25.

Codye, Corinn. *Vilma Martinez*. Milwaukee: Raintree Steck-Vaughn, 1991.

Hernandez, Al Carlo. "Vilma Martinez." *Nuestro*, August/September, 1981.

Johnson, Dean. "Chair of the Board." *Nuestro*, September, 1985.

"Leader of Latino Group Resigning." *Los Angeles Times*, December 16, 1981.

"Profile: Vilma S. Martinez." *Los Angeles Daily Journal*, January 6, 1992.

"Vilma Martinez." *California Magazine*, December, 1981.

"Vilma Martinez." *The Columbia Law Alumni Observer*, April/May, 1982.

"Vilma Martinez." *Hispanic Community Magazine*, April/May, 1988.

Barbara McClintock

Barbara McClintock (1902–1992)

I was the first woman

to receive an unshared

Nobel Prize in Medicine

for my discovery of

"jumping genes."

Have you ever wondered why the kernels on Indian corn are different colors and how they got that way? I did and, after years of research, I discovered it was caused by "jumping genes." Genes are found in the cells of all living things. All of you have genes. You inherited them from your mother and father. Your genes make you different from everyone else. They determine your hair color, your eye color, whether you're a girl or a boy, and many other things about you.

Oh, by the way, my name's Barbara McClintock and I'm a research scientist. I was born in Connecticut in 1902. My strong-minded parents taught me, along with my two sisters and my brother, to be independent and develop our own interests. Some of my interests were reading, ice skating and sitting alone thinking about things.

When I was in high school, I discovered science. I especially enjoyed mathematics and physics because I loved the challenge of working on difficult problems and finding the solutions. I wanted to go to college, but my parents were against it. My mother worried that if I became too educated, I would not be able to find a husband. Besides, my family didn't have enough money to pay for tuition.

After I graduated from high school, I got a job and helped support my family. I spent my evenings and weekends at the library educating myself. Finally, my parents saw how determined I was to go to college and they agreed to let me go.

I enrolled in Cornell University's College of Agriculture. During my junior year, I took a class in genetics. I knew then I had found an interest that would continue throughout my life.

I earned three degrees from Cornell. I studied genetics and botany. I was especially interested in studying plant cells. I became skilled at preparing cells for viewing under a microscope and always paid close attention to everything I saw. For most of my life I studied the genes of maize or "Indian corn." I spent a lot of my time

Nobel Prize-Winning Scientist

COSTUME/PROPS

Tailored shirt,
plain sweater

"Knickers," rolled up
trousers or jeans and
flat, sturdy shoes

Indian corn

Microscope

A clipboard

planting, tending and harvesting maize to supply cells for my research. It was hard work, but I loved it. I learned about the behavior of genes from the patterns on the corn kernels. By looking at the kernels, I could determine whether or not the pigment gene—the gene that controls color—was working.

When I finished my education I could not find a permanent job as a research scientist, so I continued growing and studying maize at Cornell. Later, I traveled across the country and spent six years at the University of Missouri as a junior faculty member. One summer I was invited to Cold Spring Harbor in New York to do research. I stayed for fifty years.

Cold Spring Harbor is an important research center for scientists from around the world. I was able to continue my work on maize, which led to my discovery of movable genetic elements or "jumping genes" as they are sometimes called. Jumping genes can move from one place to another within a cell and cause mutations, or changes, in new generations of plants or animals.

I presented my discovery to other scientists at Cold Spring Harbor during the summer of 1951. Most of them laughed at my findings because they were so different from what was known and accepted at that time. But I knew my findings were right and I knew eventually other scientists would understand.

Many years later, my ideas were accepted and I received many important awards. In fact, in 1983 I was the first woman to receive an unshared Nobel Prize in Medicine for my discovery of jumping genes. The Nobel Prize is the highest honor a scientist can receive.

I was happy to be recognized for a lifetime of work, but I was happiest of all doing my solitary work of growing, harvesting and studying the maize plant. "It seems a little unfair to reward a person for having so much pleasure over the years. It was fun. I couldn't wait to get up in the morning!"

NOTES/TIPS FOR PRESENTERS:

Write the word "genes" on the chalkboard.

You may want to present the monologue while sitting at a table with a microscope. As Barbara talks, you could pause, look into the microscope, jot down notes about what you just "saw."

Explain "tuition," "botany," "pigment" and "solitary."

SUGGESTED READING:

Altman, Lawrence K. "Long Island Biologist Wins Nobel in Medicine." *The New York Times*, October 11, 1983.

Arnold, Caroline. *Genetics, From Mendel to Gene Splicing*. New York: Franklin Watts, 1986.

Dash, Joan. *The Triumph of Discovery: Women Scientists Who Won the Nobel Prize*. Englewood Cliffs, New Jersey: Julian Messner, 1991.

Keller, Evelyn Fox. *A Feeling for the Organism. The Life and Work of Barbara McClintock*. New York: W. H. Freeman and Company, 1983.

Kittredge, Mary. *Barbara McClintock*. New York: Chelsea House Publishing, 1991.

Pasternak, Judy. "Barbara McClintock, 90: Nobel-Winning Geneticist." *Los Angeles Times*, September 4, 1992.

Wasson, Tyler, ed. *Nobel Prize Winners*. New York: H. W. Wilson Company, 1987.

Wilford, John N. "A Brilliant Loner in Love With Genetics." *The New York Times*, October 11, 1983.

Maria Mitchell

MARIA MITCHELL
(1818–1889)

When I was your age,

I spent many nights

looking at the stars

through a telescope.

It's going to be cold up here, but what a perfectly clear night for sweeping the skies. How many of you have ever looked at the stars through a telescope? When I was your age, I spent many nights doing just that with my father. We would climb up to the roof of our house, which we used as a little observatory, and it was up there my father taught me the wonder of the stars.

We lived on the island of Nantucket in those days. Many of our neighbors were sailors and captains from whaling ships. We all knew how important the stars were in helping the ships find their way at sea. Captains came to my father to have their instruments set correctly, so they would not get lost or have a shipwreck. He taught me how to do it, too. This meant doing very hard math problems, but I liked doing them.

For a while, I was a school teacher. Then I became the librarian for our town. It was the perfect job for me. When there were no questions to answer, I could read as much as I wanted.

Did you see that? [*Point into the distant sky*.] It looked like a shooting star. Tonight reminds me of a night when I was 29. I had come home tired from working at the library. My parents were having a small party, but I just wanted to go up to the telescope on the roof. I was looking in the area of the North Star when I thought I saw a small blurry spot I had never noticed before. Since I knew that part of the sky like I knew Main Street, Nantucket, I was sure I had not seen that spot before. I wrote down the time, 10:30 p.m., in my notebook and the exact location. Then I ran to get my father. He looked through the telescope and checked the star charts. "It's a comet!" he said, and gave me a big hug. "You have discovered a comet above the North Star."

Did you know that if you are the first person to see a comet, it is named in your honor? Because of my discovery, I received a special gold medal from the King of Denmark. It had my name,

ASTRONOMER

Maria (mah-RYE-ah) Mitchell, and the date, October 1, 1847, on one side. On the other side it said, "Not in vain do we watch the setting and rising of the stars."

I was invited to Boston where I was made the first woman member of the American Academy of Arts and Sciences. A reporter asked me if it was true I watched the stars all night, then slept until sundown the next day. I told him that in our house we all got up at half-past six in the morning. Then he asked if it was good for a woman's health to lose so much sleep. I pointed out that my mother lost more sleep staying up nights with her nine babies.

After my mother passed away and all my brothers and sisters were married, my father and I moved off the island. We were barely settled when I received an invitation to teach astronomy at a new college for women called Vassar. I was nervous because I had never been to college myself. But my father thought it would be a wonderful opportunity to tell others about the stars.

On the first day of class I told my students, "I cannot expect to make you astronomers, but I do expect to make you think." I got in trouble at times. I did not like giving grades. I could not see how you could measure someone's mind. One night, I had a tree cut down because it was blocking my view of an important comet. The next morning they were calling me George Washington. But I continued to teach at Vassar for twenty-two years.

It's been very nice talking with you. Please excuse me now, I must get back to my work before it gets light.

COSTUME/PROPS

Warm Victorian dress

Telescope

Astronomy books

Flashlight inside black box with star-shaped openings

NOTES/TIPS FOR PRESENTERS:

Mitchell was strong-featured, almost stern-looking, with dark eyes. She was shy, and at 31, still wore her black hair in curls. Mitchell did not like to speak in public and disliked having her picture taken.

Turn off lights in classroom. Sit and look through a telescope.

Show students where Nantucket, Massachusetts, is on a map.

Encourage students to look up comets that have been discovered by others.

SUGGESTED READING:

Baker, Rachel and Joanna Baker Merlen. *America's First Woman Astronomer: Maria Mitchell*. New York: Simon and Schuster, 1960.

Howe, M. A. DeWolfe. *A Baker's Dozen of Historic New England Houses and Their Occupants*. Little, Brown & Co., 1951.

Kendall, Phebe Mitchell. *Maria Mitchell: Life, Letters and Journals*. Boston: Lee and Shepard, 1896.

McPherson, Stephanie Sanmartino. *Rooftop Astronomer: A Story about Maria Mitchell*. Minneapolis: Carolrhoda Books, Inc., 1990.

Morgan, Helen L. *Maria Mitchell: First Lady of American Astronomy*. Philadelphia: Westminster Press, 1977.

Wayne, Bennett, ed. *Women Who Dared to be Different*. Champaign, Illinois: Carrard Publishing Company, 1973.

Julia
Morgan

JULIA MORGAN (1872–1957)

I thought designing

a building would

be exciting and

challenging.

I am Julia Morgan, an architect. I designed more than 700 buildings in my lifetime. Because my parents encouraged me to get an education, I studied math and physics while other girls thought about parties and dresses. What was funny was that my sister and I got better grades than any of our three brothers.

Our parents gave each of us jobs to teach us responsibility. One of my jobs was to polish the wooden stair railings. I often wondered why railings had to have so many fancy designs on them which took a long time to dust. I knew that if I were designing them, I would make them smooth and easy to clean.

In the 1880s, most girls got married after high school, but when I graduated, I enrolled in college. I studied math and science—my favorite subjects. Sometimes I was the only woman in the class. During this time, I decided I wanted to be an architect. I thought designing a building would be exciting and challenging, like figuring out a complicated problem step by step. I knew that once it was finished, I would have something to be proud of that would last a long time.

After I graduated from the University of California at Berkeley in 1894, I spent four years studying architecture and French until I could continue my studies at an architectural school in Paris, France. I became the first woman to be admitted to the École des Beaux-Arts (ay-KOHL day bohz-AR) in Paris.

I returned to California and set up an office in the garage of my parents' house. I began designing new houses for friends and neighbors, and also worked for an architect who was designing new buildings at the University of California at Berkeley. We used reinforced concrete, which has steel rods going through it to make it stronger. It had not been used in California before.

In 1904, I became the first woman licensed as an architect in California and was able to open my own office in San Francisco. In 1906, a terrible earthquake struck San Francisco, destroying 28,000 buildings. People soon discovered that buildings built with

ARCHITECT

reinforced concrete were still standing. I was asked to rebuild the Fairmont Hotel, a beautiful hotel on top of a hill.

From that time on, I was very busy. I built churches and schools. My favorite school design was one in which each classroom had a door going directly outside. Until then, most schools had long halls or staircases, but I wanted children to be able to get outdoors to play as quickly as possible.

I never married or had children, but I loved them, and whenever I built a house, I added something special just for the children: sometimes a secret closet, or a hidden stairway, or a playhouse. I wanted children to remember their childhood as a happy time.

One day, a famous publisher named William Randolph Hearst asked me to build him a grand house in San Simeon, California. Mr. Hearst owned furniture and paintings he had collected from old castles in Europe and he wanted a place to put them. It took twenty years to build what Mr. Hearst called "The Ranch," but what we know as Hearst Castle. It had 165 rooms and the largest private zoo in the world.

Later, I built another property in California for Mr. Hearst called Wyntoon. It had cottages named after fairy tales: Cinderella, Bear House and Sleeping Beauty. I continued to design buildings until I was 79 years old. "My buildings will be my legacy; they will speak for me long after I am gone."

COSTUME/PROPS

Suit with a ruffled blouse, hat

Hair worn simply and smoothly, or in a bun

Pictures of Hearst Castle, the Fairmont Hotel or other buildings by Morgan

Blueprints, drafting tools

NOTES/TIPS TO PRESENTERS:

Show and explain the different views in blueprints.

Display pictures of buildings damaged or destroyed by an earthquake.

Compare the 1906 San Francisco earthquake with a more recent one.

Show pictures of buildings designed by Morgan. Many of these can be found in the book by Sara Holmes Boutelle.

SUGGESTED READING:

Boutelle, Sara Holmes. *Julia Morgan, Architect*. New York: Abbeville Press Publishers, 1988.

James, Cary. *Julia Morgan*. New York: Chelsea House Publishers, 1990.

Wadsworth, Ginger. *Julia Morgan, Architect of Dreams*. Minneapolis: Lerner Publishing Co., 1990.

ALICE PAUL

ALICE PAUL
(1885–1977)

Did you ever believe in something so much you were willing to do anything, even go to jail and go on a hunger strike, to help people realize you were right? Well, I did. My name is Alice Stokes Paul and I spent my life working for equality for women.

I was born in 1885 in Moorestown, New Jersey. My family was Quaker and we believed in equal rights for all people. I always worked very hard and my father often said, "When there is anything hard or disagreeable to be done, I bank on Alice."

Learning and helping others was always an important part of my life. When I was young, girls often were not allowed to go to college, but I did. I attended five colleges and received six degrees. I went to England to study and to work with poor families. While I was there, I became friends with Mrs. Pankhurst and other English suffragists. In those days, only men were allowed to vote. Suffragists believed all people should vote, women as well as men. I agreed with the suffragists and so I worked to help them change the laws in England.

When I came home to the United States, I was still interested in women's right to vote, so my friend Lucy Burns and I decided to work to pass a law called a constitutional amendment to make it legal for women to vote in our own country.

When we started our work, women could vote in only five states. I organized demonstrations and thousands of people came to Washington, D.C., to show their support for women's right to vote. Large demonstrations with people from all over the country were unusual then. We did things to call attention to our message. We always wore sashes and carried banners that were purple, white and gold. Everyone throughout the country knew a purple, white and gold flag stood for women's suffrage.

When the President and Congress did not respond, we began to picket the White House. For over a year, women walked in front of the President's house carrying flags and banners with quotes about democracy, such as, "Mr. President, how long must women

Profiles of Women Past & Present

WOMEN'S SUFFRAGE LEADER

wait for liberty?" We picketed every day, rain or shine. People often came to help us. When it was very cold, they brought us hot bricks to stand on so we could keep warm. The tour buses included us as a part of their tours of the important sights of Washington. People began to respect that we really believed in a woman's right to vote.

However, things changed and many of the picketers began to be arrested and put in jail. The conditions in jail were awful. Often the food they gave us had gone bad. One time we held a contest to see who could find the most maggots in our dinner. One woman found fifteen! To protest these injustices, we went on a hunger strike. After a few days, the guards at the prison held us down and forced tubes through our noses and down our throats to give us food. It was a horrible experience and we all got quite sick. But we did not give up. We just kept working and trying new ways to convince the government. Women from all over the country came to help and we often gave them jobs they did not think they could do. But I knew they could do more than they thought they could. And they did.

In May of 1919, Congress passed the Suffrage Amendment and a little over one year later, women voted in every state. This victory was important to women, but I did not believe it was enough. In 1923, I wrote another amendment called the Equal Rights Amendment (ERA), which would require the government to treat men and women equally. It has not passed yet, but I believe some day it will.

We need to be concerned about people in all parts of the world. That is why I worked to have the United Nations and other international groups believe in equality for men and women.

I lived to be 92 years old. I think that qualifies me to give you young people some advice: "If you believe in something, keep working to make it happen. You will succeed if you work hard and don't give up."

COSTUME/PROPS

Early 20th Century white dress

Sash across one shoulder fastened at the opposite hip (striped with one stripe each of gold, white and purple)

Banners or flags of the same colors with messages such as: "Liberty is a fundamental demand of the human spirit" and "How long must women wait for liberty?"

NOTES/TIPS FOR PRESENTERS:

Paul was a tiny woman. She was quiet and serene, yet persuasive. Even though she masterminded the suffrage movement for years, she was rarely in the spotlight and not often photographed.

The Office of the National Woman's Party, which Paul founded, is located at 144 Constitution Avenue, Washington, D.C. They maintain a large library and are available by phone to answer queries.

Explain "picketing."

Discuss whether girls should be allowed to go to college.

Ask: "What things are still not equal for women?"

SUGGESTED READING:

Ford, Linda G. *Iron-Jawed Angels: The Suffrage Militancy of the National Woman's Party, 1912–1920*. Lanham, Maryland: University Press of America, 1991.

Irwin, I. H. *The Story of Alice Paul and the National Woman's Party*. Fairfax, Virginia: Denlinger's Publishers, Ltd., 1977.

Lunardini, Christine A. *From Equal Suffrage to Equal Rights: Alice Paul and the National Woman's Party, 1910–1928*. New York: New York University Press, 1986.

O'Neill, W.L. *Everyone Was Brave: A History of Feminism in America*. Chicago: Quadrangle Books, 1971.

Rothe, A., ed. *Current Biography, Who's News and Why*. New York: H.W. Wilson Co., 1947.

ANNIE SMITH PECK

ANNIE SMITH PECK (1850–1935)

My interest in mountain

climbing began

the first time I saw

the Matterhorn in

Switzerland.

My name is Annie Smith Peck. I was born in Radcliffe, Rhode Island, on October 19, 1850, the only daughter in my family. I loved the physical challenges of sports, but my four older brothers seldom allowed me to join their games. I practiced hard, determined to be even better at sports than they were.

All my brothers attended college, so naturally I wanted to go too. I went to the University of Michigan and graduated with honors in every subject. I taught for several years and was one of the first women in the United States to become a college professor.

My interest in mountain climbing began the first time I saw the Matterhorn in Switzerland. I was seized with a determination to climb it one day. To prepare myself, I spent the next ten years climbing smaller mountains and learning mountaineering skills. My first climb was Mount Shasta in California in 1888. When I climbed the summit of the Matterhorn in 1895, I was instantly famous, both for my endurance and courage and my "unladylike" climbing attire.

I gave up teaching in 1892 and began to support myself by giving talks about my adventures. Determined to conquer "some height where no man had previously stood," I became interested in climbing unexplored mountains of South America. Five times, I tried, unsuccessfully, to climb Mount Huascarán (wahs-kah-RAHN) in the Andes Mountains of Peru. At the time, it was thought to be the highest mountain in the Americas.

In 1908, when I was 58 years old, I attempted to climb Huascarán for the sixth time. I hired two experienced Swiss guides and four porters to carry our equipment. Since we would face bitter cold temperatures during the climb, I took everything from two woolen face masks and fur mittens to woolen underwear and tights. My hiking boots were four sizes larger than my regular shoes to make room for heavy stockings.

We began our expedition by riding on burros for several hours before camping for the night. The next morning, the moun-

MOUNTAINEER

tains were covered with clouds, so I postponed our climb. The third day, we hiked to the snow line and set up our camp. The next two days we climbed across the glacier between the two high peaks of Huascarán. We wore boots studded with nails to grip the ice. The next day, we almost had to turn back when the porter carrying our stove fell down into a deep crevasse. Luckily, we rescued him and the stove.

On the sixth day, we began our final climb to the summit. It was back-breaking work. We had to cut steps with an ice ax most of the way. We rested often because of the high winds and altitude. By late afternoon, we were almost at the summit. One of the guides and I stopped to try to measure the altitude. After a few minutes, we gave up and looked for the other guide. I was furious when I learned he had climbed to the summit ahead of me. By tradition, the honor of reaching the summit first should have been mine as organizer of the expedition.

I swallowed my anger and climbed up to the summit. I wanted to stay there for a while, but there was no time. It was almost dark and we still had to go back down. It took us nearly three hours of slipping, sliding and falling on the rocks and ice to reach our camp. We were so tired that we rested for an entire day before starting back down the mountain.

I was world famous after climbing Huascarán. The government of Peru gave me a gold medal and named the north peak "Huascarán Cumbre Ana Peck" in my honor. Although it was later discovered that Huascarán was not the highest peak in the Americas, my expedition was the first to conquer the summit.

I traveled and climbed mountains all my life. I never got married and never settled down in one place. I was a suffragist because I believed women should have the right to vote.

When I climbed Mount Coropuna in Peru, I planted a "Votes for Women" flag at the summit. My last climb was Mount Madison in New Hampshire when I was 82 years old.

COSTUME/PROPS

Hip length sweater or tunic

Heavy canvas "knickers"

High leather boots

Canvas or felt hat tied with a scarf under chin

Ice ax, climber's rope

Replica of a gold medal from Peruvian government

NOTES/TIPS FOR PRESENTERS:

When Peck spoke to audiences, people were often surprised by her appearance, not expecting a woman mountain climber to be so very small and feminine in her dress.

You might want to locate pictures of the Matterhorn, Mount Shasta, Huascarán or any of the other mountains Peck climbed.

Explain why more rest is needed at high altitudes (less oxygen).

Have students research the highest peak in the Americas.

A "Votes for Women" flag or banner might prompt a classroom discussion of the suffrage movement.

SUGGESTED READING:

Hindley, Geoffrey. *The Roof of the World.* Vol. 15 of *The Marshall Cavendish Illustrated Encyclopedia of Discovery and Exploration.* New York: Marshall Cavendish, 1990.

Peavy, Linda and Ursula Smith. *Women Who Changed Things, Nine Lives that Made a Difference.* New York: Charles Scribner's Sons, 1983.

Rappaport, Doreen. *Living Dangerously. American Women Who Risked Their Lives for Adventure.* New York: Harper Collins, 1991.

Thomas, Lowell. *Lowell Thomas' Book of the High Mountains.* New York: Julian Messner, Inc., 1964.

Susan LaFlesche Picotte

SUSAN LAFLESCHE PICOTTE (1865–1915)

I was the first American

Indian woman

to become a

medical doctor.

Have you ever lived someplace where everyone was different from you? It can be lonely, can't it? That's how I felt many times during my life. I was the first American Indian woman to become a medical doctor, and I often traveled far from my home in Nebraska. I am Susan LaFlesche (lah-FLESH) Picotte (pee-COT).

I was born on the Omaha Reservation in 1865 during a time when our traditional ways were changing forever. My father was Joseph "Iron Eye" LaFlesche, chief of the Omahas. My mother, Mary, was called "The One Woman." I had a brother and three sisters. My oldest sister, Suzette, was called "Bright Eyes," but she was the only one of us given an Omaha name because my father believed we would have to adopt the "white ways" to survive.

My father tried to give the Omahas an example to follow. He built us a wood frame house, became a farmer and sent my sisters and me to the reservation school to learn to read and write in English. At the same time, he often questioned the authority of the reservation agent and fought against any laws which would be unfair to the Omahas. I often stood at my father's side as he helped and advised his people. All of my life, I tried to follow his example.

When I was 14, my sister Marguerite and I attended the Institute for Young Ladies in New Jersey. We returned home three years later and I became a teacher. Once, I helped the reservation doctor take care of a sick woman. I started thinking about doing something to help my people stay strong and healthy. Maybe I could do a better job than the reservation doctor, who sometimes didn't seem to care whether he helped us or not.

Later, Marguerite and I attended a college in Virginia. While there, I met Dr. Martha M. Waldron, one of the first woman doctors in the United States and decided I would become a doctor. At my graduation, I said: "The shores of success can only be reached by crossing the bridge of faith, and I shall try hard." I would try to help the Omahas cross to a new way of life.

First Native American Woman Medical Doctor

I attended the Women's Medical College in Philadelphia. Marguerite didn't go with me, so I felt very homesick at first. But soon, I was busy with my studies. I was the first American Indian many people in Philadelphia had ever seen. They were curious about me, so I was often invited to meetings and parties where I made many friends.

I finished medical school at the age of 24. I returned home and became the reservation school doctor. Later, I was appointed doctor for the whole reservation. I had to take care of over a thousand people. Many times I had to ride on horseback to the homes of sick people. During the winters, I thought I would freeze to death as I rode across the snow-covered prairie. After only four years, I had to retire because my health was failing.

In 1894, I married Henry Picotte, a Sioux Indian. Soon we had two sons and I was healthy enough to practice medicine again. My office was in our home, and every night I put a lamp in our front window to light the way for anyone who needed my help.

When Henry died in 1905, my sons and I moved to Walthill, a new town on the reservation. I worked to improve health laws and solve the growing problem of alcoholism on the reservation. Once I wrote in my diary that, besides doctoring, I did everything from settling arguments to naming babies. I even traveled to Washington, D. C., to help change laws unfair to the Omahas. It seemed as if I had become the unofficial "chief" of the Omahas.

For many years I dreamed of building a hospital on the reservation. Finally, with the support of the Presbyterian Board of Missions and the people of Walthill, my dream came true. When the hospital opened in 1913, I was put in charge.

I died in 1915 when I was only 50 years old. At my funeral, the closing prayer was offered by an Omaha in my native language.

COSTUME/PROPS

Long, simple, frontier-style dress or long skirt and blouse

Long heavy coat, thick shawl and muffler

Medical equipment (bottles and thermometers) packed in saddlebag

Antique-style lamp or lantern

NOTES/TIPS FOR PRESENTERS:

The term "Indian" is used in this monologue as that is how Picotte referred to herself, her family and the Omahas. The term "Native American" is used now.

In photographs of Picotte, she is usually shown wearing frontier-style clothing. In portraying this woman stereotypical "Indian costumes" should not be used.

Point out Omaha on a map.

Explain what alcoholism is.

Discuss why the Omahas "would have to adopt the 'white ways' to survive."

SUGGESTED READING:

Bataille, Gretchen A., ed. *Native American Women. A Biographical Dictionary*. New York: Garland Publishing, 1993.

Ferris, Jeri. *Native American Doctor: The Story of Susan LaFlesche Picotte*. Minneapolis: Carolrhoda Books, Inc., 1991.

WILMA RUDOLPH

WILMA RUDOLPH (1940–1994)

My name is Wilma Rudolph. When I was born on June 23, 1940, my parents never dreamed I would someday be the "fastest woman on earth." I was born two months early and weighed only four and a half pounds, so they worried I might not survive. I grew up in Clarksville, Tennessee. My parents worked hard to support me and my seven brothers and sisters, as well as my fourteen half-siblings. We lived in a small house without electricity or an indoor bathroom, and my mother made our clothes out of old flour sacks.

I got very sick when I was four and almost died from double pneumonia and scarlet fever. When I got better, my right leg was crooked and I couldn't move it. A doctor said I had also had polio, a disease that destroys the nerves which tell the muscles what to do. He said I might not ever walk again. My mother didn't believe him, and every week for four years we rode a bus to a hospital for treatments to make my leg stronger. She learned to do the treatments, and she and my older sisters and brothers took turns rubbing and exercising my leg four times a day.

By the time I was 6, I was able to walk by wearing a special metal leg brace. I couldn't go to school, so my father hired a tutor to teach me at home. I finally started school when I was 7, but the other children made fun of me because of my brace. "I became determined to do something none of them would ever do so they'd have to accept me."

I regained full use of my leg when I was 11. After years of always watching from the sidelines, I went out for basketball and track. When I ran in track meets, I always came in first. But one time, I went to a meet at a college and lost every race. I knew then I had a lot to learn.

That summer, I went to a track program at Tennessee State University. Coach Ed Temple taught me about running and helped me develop mental toughness. At the end of the summer, I tried out for the 1956 Summer Olympic team. Before the trials, I was so nervous I couldn't eat! But I made the team and at the age of 16, won

Profiles of Women Past & Present

OLYMPIC GOLD MEDALIST

a bronze medal in the women's 400-meter relay in Melbourne, Australia.

In 1957, I enrolled at Tennessee State University, the first person in my family to go to college. I joined the "Tigerbelles" track team and worked hard to keep up my grades.

I made the 1960 Summer Olympic team and went to Rome, Italy, determined to "win at least one or two gold medals for myself and my country." Even though I twisted my ankle during practice and couldn't run for a few days, I won the qualifying races for the women's 100- and 200-meter dashes. In the finals, I won two gold medals.

The last event was the 400-meter relay. I was the "anchor," so I ran the last "leg" of the race. As my teammate handed me the baton, I almost dropped it. That would have cost us the race. Suddenly, all of my training was put to the test. I sprinted hard, stretching to cross the finish line first. The race was so close the judges had to look at photographs to decide who won. My team won, setting a new Olympic record. I became the first American woman to win three gold medals in one Olympics.

When I came back home, everyone, black and white, cheered and waved at a parade in my honor. This was the first integrated event in the history of Clarksville. In 1962, I received the Babe Didrikson Zaharias Award, which is given to the most outstanding female athlete in the world. That same year, I retired from competition while I was still a winner.

I graduated from Tennessee State and became a teacher, a track coach and a mother of four. I believed it was important to give something back to sports and to people, so I founded the Wilma Rudolph Foundation in 1981 to provide free training for young athletes. I always enjoyed talking with young people about the challenges and successes in my life. "My. . . life is an example of what a person can achieve, even if he or she comes from a family of twenty-two children and has to overcome illness and hardship."

COSTUME/PROPS

Sleeveless U.S.A. shirt and shorts, warm-up suit, running shoes

Three gold medals

Athletic bag

NOTES/TIPS FOR PRESENTERS:

In the various sources consulted for this monologue, there is conflicting information regarding which of Rudolph's legs was paralyzed. According to her autobiography, her right leg was paralyzed. Rudolph died of brain cancer at the age of 54.

Show a leg brace similar to the one Rudolph wore as a child.

Measure 100 and 200 meters on the school playground and have the students run the dash.

Obtain a copy of *Wilma*, the movie based on Rudolph's autobiography.

Discuss segregation during the years Rudolph was growing up. Explain "integrated."

Discuss the origin of the Olympic Games.

SUGGESTED READING:

Biracree, Tom. *Wilma Rudolph*. New York: Chelsea House Publishers, 1988.

Hendershott, Jon. *Track's Greatest Women*. Los Altos, California: Tafnews Press, 1987.

McHenry, Robert. *Liberty's Women*. Springfield, Mass: G. & C. Merriam Company, 1980.

Rudolph, Wilma (with Martin Rolbovsky). *Wilma*. New American Library, 1977.

Wolff, Alexander and Richard O'Brien, eds. "Fast Train from Clarksville." *Sports Illustrated*, November 21, 1994.

Yoshiko Uchida

YOSHIKO UCHIDA (1921–1992)

I grew up in Berkeley, California. My parents were born in Japan, but my sister and I were born in California. We were proud to be American, but when people saw me, they usually saw only my Japanese face. Teachers had a problem pronouncing my name, Yoshiko (YOSH-ko) Uchida (Oo-CHEE-da), even when I shortened it to Yoshi.

I started writing when we got our first puppy. I bought a notebook and wrote down everything he did. I also started a diary and wrote down everything that happened to me. Soon I discovered how much fun it was to write, and at 10, I wrote my first story, "Jimmy Chipmunk." By 12, I had written my first book.

When I was 16, I entered college. Just before I graduated, Japan bombed Hawaii. This meant war between Japan and the United States. Men from the government, called FBI agents, took my father away for questioning. Another FBI man sat in our living room, watching us. I was horrified when Mama made tea for him. My father was taken to a prisoner-of-war camp in Montana.

Suddenly all Japanese people in the United States were considered "enemy aliens," even those of us who were American citizens. We had not done anything wrong; we just looked like the enemy. People were rude to us and thought all Japanese had started this terrible war. Soon, the United States government decided to lock us all up in internment camps. We had to leave our nice house with its flower garden and fruit trees, and get rid of everything we owned. We even had to give away our dog.

Armed guards took us in buses to an assembly center at a big racetrack surrounded by barbed wire fence. My mother, my sister and I were assigned a horse stall to live in. That stall was big enough for only one horse. It was dark and cold and smelly in there. Later, my father was returned to us from Montana and we were a family again.

My sister and I taught school in the center. Every day, our students recited the Pledge of Allegiance to the flag of the United

WRITER

States, even though we were thought of as enemy aliens. Guards watched us all day. We had to be in our stall every night at six o'clock for roll call. We were never alone. We wanted to get out of that place.

When we finally did, it was only to be relocated to an internment camp in the middle of a desert in Utah called Topaz. There were 8,000 Japanese people in that camp. The wind blew fiercely there and whenever it did, dirt and sand covered everything.

I taught second grade at the camp. When I saw my classroom for the first time, I was shocked. There was a big hole in the roof, no tables, no chairs, no books and no heat. Many children got sick.

After a while, some people were allowed to leave Topaz if they could prove they were not dangerous and had a job. When I won a scholarship to college and my sister got a job, we were able to go. It was sad to leave our parents, but they were happy for us.

After I earned my master's degree from college, I became a school teacher in Philadelphia. When my parents were allowed to leave the internment camp, my sister and I found an apartment for them and we all lived together again.

When I visited Japan as an adult, I discovered its beauty. I wanted to tell other Japanese Americans about their own history, so I wrote a book about the first Japanese settlers in America. I also wrote books about the internment camps.

Forty years after the war, President Gerald Ford announced: "Not only was the evacuation wrong, but Japanese Americans were and are loyal Americans." I hope my books will remind people of what happened so they will never allow it to happen again. We must always remember that freedom is our most precious possession.

COSTUME/PROPS

A skirt and blouse or a suit

Books written by Uchida

A picture of an internment camp

NOTES/TIPS TO PRESENTERS:

Uchida's father was a businessman. Her mother wrote poetry and made dresses for Yoshiko and her older sister Keiko. Uchida worked for a short time as a teacher, but then became a secretary so that she would have more time for her writing. She wrote thirty books, many stories and won prizes for her work. She never married, and died of a stroke in 1992.

Discuss internment of Japanese Americans during World War II. Compare with treatment of German Americans.

SUGGESTED READING:

Marvis, Barbara J. *Contemporary American Success Stories. Famous People of Asian Ancestry*. Vol. II. Childs, Maryland: Mitchell Lane Publishers, 1994.

Uchida, Yoshiko. *The Dancing Kettle and Other Japanese Folk Tales*. New York: Harcourt, 1949.

Uchida, Yoshiko. *The Magic Listening Cap: More Folk Tales from Japan*. Berkeley: Creative Arts Book Co., 1955.

Uchida, Yoshiko. *Sumi's Prize*. New York: Scribner, 1964.

Uchida, Yoshiko. *The Sea of Gold, and Other Tales from Japan*. New York: Scribner, 1965.

Uchida, Yoshiko. *Journey to Topaz*. New York: Scribner, 1971.

Uchida, Yoshiko. *Samurai of Gold Hill*. New York: Scribner, 1972.

Uchida, Yoshiko. *A Jar of Dreams*. New York: Atheneum, 1981.

Uchida, Yoshiko. *Desert Exile*. University of Washington Press, 1982.

Uchida, Yoshiko. *The Best Bad Thing*. New York: Atheneum, 1983.

Uchida, Yoshiko. *The Happiest Ending*. New York: Atheneum, 1985.

Uchida, Yoshiko. *The Invisible Thread*. New York: Julian Messner/ Simon & Schuster, 1991.

MARIAN ANDERSON
(1902–1993)

Do you think that people with great talent grow up and become famous just because they are good at soccer or music? Well, as I found out, it takes a lot of study and practice. I had a beautiful voice, so I became a concert singer. My name is Marian Anderson.

I was born in Philadelphia in 1902. At that time, black people were not allowed the same privileges as white people. I first sang in our church choir when I was 6, and sometimes we traveled on trains to sing in churches in other cities. But in Southern states, we could not stay in a hotel or eat in some restaurants because of our dark skin.

When I was small, we didn't have much money, and people in our community raised money to pay for my singing lessons. I worked hard and became skilled enough to enter a singing contest. The prize was a chance to sing at a big concert hall in New York City, and I won!

At 21, I went on a concert tour in Europe. People there liked me very much and didn't seem to care about my dark skin. I learned the songs that they liked to hear and I brought American music to them. One of the hardest things I had to learn was to sing in three other languages: Italian, Spanish and German.

Back in the United States, I sang outdoors in front of the Lincoln Memorial and over 75,000 people came to hear me. I felt greatly honored to sing at Abraham Lincoln's Memorial because he had done so much to help black people when he was President.

I continued to sing in cities around the world, and my concerts were always packed. Eventually, I could stay in hotels wherever I wished, but it bothered me that other black people were not treated as fairly. Just as people had once helped me, I finally had enough money to help many young singers pay for their music lessons.

Because of my successful singing career and because I cared so much about equality for all people, I became one of the most admired women in the world. I was given a special Congressional Medal, and the United Nations Peace Prize. I lived to be 91 years old, proud of my contributions to music and worldwide peace and understanding. The medal I received reads, "Marian Anderson has ennobled her race and her country, while her voice has enthralled the world."

MAYA ANGELOU
(1928–   )

My name is Maya Angelou (AN-jel-oh). I was born in 1928 in Missouri. When I was 3 years old and my brother Bailey was 4, our parents sent us to live with our grandmother. We were put on a train by ourselves with a tag attached to our wrists.

In those days we went to schools separate from those for white people and lived in different neighborhoods. One time, when I had a bad toothache, the white dentist told my grandmother that he would not take care of a Negro, so we had to ride a bus to another town to find a dentist to help me.

Our grandmother taught Bailey and me to work hard and to trust in God. Bailey was my best friend. He gave me the name Maya because when he was little he used to call me "mine" and it sounded like Maya.

When I was a teenager, I moved to San Francisco to live with my mother. After high school, I had many jobs. I was everything from a cook to a night club dancer and singer. I also became the first black woman conductor on the San Francisco streetcar.

In the 1960s, I joined the Civil Rights Movement and worked with the Reverend Dr. Martin Luther King Jr. During that time, I wrote a play called *Cabaret for Freedom* to raise money for our cause.

Later, I married a man who was from Africa and we moved there. In Africa, we realized it was the "first time in our lives when the color of our skin was accepted as correct and normal." I worked as a writer and editor there, which was unusual because women in Africa were not often allowed to work at jobs outside their homes.

Since that time, I have written many poems, plays, songs and books about my life. *I Know Why The Caged Bird Sings* is the story of my childhood and has been made into a movie. My film, *Georgia, Georgia,* was the first movie ever written by an African American woman.

In recent years I have been honored many times. In 1992, President-elect Clinton asked me to write a poem to read at his inauguration. I am a director, a lecturer and a teacher. I now teach at a university in North Carolina. I live by the rule that my mother and grandmother taught me when I was small: "You may encounter many defeats, but you must not be defeated."

JUDITH BACA
(1946–   )

Mi abuela, my grandmother, believed that people who hurt others had been badly hurt themselves. Sometimes, people would stare at her because she looked like an Apache Indian with her long dark braids. But she was not an Apache; she was from Mexico. Once a store owner tried to cheat her by giving her the wrong change and he was very rude to her. But my grandmother was kind to him anyway. She taught me to treat everybody with respect.

Me llamo, my name, is Judith Baca and I am an artist and activist. That means I believe taking art to people *es muy importante*, is very important, and can change how people think about others. I was born in California in 1946 and am a Chicana, which means that *mi familia*, my family, came from the country of Mexico. I paint murals and help others organize mural painting in their neighborhoods. A mural is a large picture painted right on a wall.

I started to paint when I was in kindergarten. Because I spoke English poorly, my kindergarten teacher would let me sit in a corner and paint. Once I started painting, I found a way to express myself without words. At home there was no extra money to buy paints but my mother proudly displayed all my art.

After I graduated from college, I taught art at parks and schools in Los Angeles. I began to notice that kids who hung out at parks used art to express themselves—with their tattoos, special clothing and graffiti. I decided to form a group of *muchachos*, boys and girls, ages 14 to 20, and together we painted a mural on a wall at a local park. The kids were from different gangs and neighborhoods but had found a way to work together.

Later, I helped develop over 250 murals painted around Los Angeles and started a public art center called SPARC, which is known worldwide.

One of my projects is a movable mural about peace and cooperation called "The World Wall: A Vision of the Future Without Fear." I feel it is important for people to imagine world peace if we can ever hope for it to happen. As this mural goes to each country around the world, artists paint their vision of peace on it.

Today, I teach classes on murals and public art at a university. My latest project will use doorways and bridges to show different cultures of our city. It will be like a big "show and tell" explaining why people are different and what makes them the same. As my grandmother taught me when I was a little girl, when we learn to accept others, we stop spreading hate and start spreading peace.

SUSAN BUTCHER
(1954–   )

Can you imagine living in a log cabin in Alaska and taking care of 150 dogs every day? Well, I really do have 150 dogs, mostly Huskies, and I raise them for dogsled racing, or "mushing," as it is called in Alaska. I won a famous Sled Dog Race called the Iditarod four times. My name is Susan Butcher.

I haven't always lived in Alaska. I was born in Massachusetts. Even when I was young, I did not like city living. I wanted my parents to tear down our house and build a tiny log cabin so there would be more room for grass and trees.

When I was in school, I enjoyed sports. After I graduated from high school, I worked for an animal doctor. One day, I read about the very first Iditarod Sled Dog Race, 1,000 miles long, that would cross over icy land, frozen rivers, thick forests and tall mountains. I was very excited about it and knew that someday I would race in it.

A few years later, I moved to Alaska and bought several dogs. I lived in a small cabin in the Alaskan wilderness, and the only way to reach my cabin was by plane. I chopped firewood, got my water from a creek, and hunted for food. After running my dogs, I would rub their sore muscles. I treated my dogs with love and respect. I learned to trust them when we were on runs, and they learned they could depend on me. My dogs became my family and my friends.

I entered the Iditarod for the first time in 1978. During the race in 1985, my dog team and I came upon a moose blocking the trail. The moose charged and began to attack my dogs. I grabbed my ax and went after that moose. I fought hard to save my dogs. Finally, another musher came along and shot the moose. Two of my dogs died and I had to drop out of the race.

After so many years of trying to win and experiencing the moose attack, you might think I would not want to race again. But I did, and the next year, in 1986, I won the Iditarod in record-breaking time! I won again in 1987 and 1988, becoming the first person to win three Iditarod races in a row.

I love everything about the Iditarod: the mountain views, the wild animals and the long trails. I'm really happy when I'm out there mushing or caring for my dogs. "The Iditarod is something that was made for me."

JULIETTE GORDON LOW
(1860–1927)

When I was a child, I liked to act out the stories my grandmother told us about her adventures in the wilderness. I never tired of that world of make-believe and adventure, and when I grew up, I kept that world open for many girls and their grown-up leaders.

My name is Juliette Gordon Low and I founded of the Girl Scouts of the U.S.A. I was an active child, and my sister Nellie called me "Crazy Daisy" because I enjoyed making up games, writing and acting in plays, and playing with my pet animals.

My parents sent me to boarding school and then finishing school in New York City. That school was so strict that we were required to speak only French and were never allowed outside the building except in the company of our teachers.

After I finished my schooling, I traveled a lot and met William Low, a wealthy businessman. We got married and left on our honeymoon, but had to return two days later because a piece of wedding rice had become stuck in my ear. When the doctor tried to remove it, I became totally deaf in that ear. I was already partially deaf in my other ear, but I was not the kind of person to be stopped by a handicap.

Once we settled in England, we lived very well. We traveled all over the world, socializing with nobility and celebrities.

When my husband died in 1905, I continued to travel, and in 1911 I met Sir Robert Baden-Powell. He told me about his work with the Boy Scouts and also about the Girl Guide program he had started. I was so excited that within weeks I had started a Girl Guide company. I traveled to America to start Girl Guiding there. I had found a purpose in my life, and was the happiest I had ever been. I gave girls a chance to play basketball, take nature hikes, go camping and learn about boys and girls in other lands.

I founded the Girl Scouts of the U.S.A. in 1913. I was sure that Girl Scouting could make the world a better place. I helped start camps for girls and leaders, designed an official uniform and wrote a guide book. I brought girls from other countries to the United States for the World Camp. I wanted scouts from around the world to think of each other as friends and neighbors.

I died in 1927 and was buried in my full uniform, with a tin cup and knife at my belt. In my pocket was a telegram from Girl Scout Headquarters that read, "You are not only the first Girl Scout, but the best Girl Scout of them all."

WILMA MANKILLER (1945–)

I am Wilma Pearl Mankiller and from 1985 to 1994 I was the Principal Chief of the Cherokee Nation. My job as chief was like that of all leaders: to help the Cherokee people take care of themselves and their families, be healthy, have jobs and be safe.

I was born in 1945 in Oklahoma. When I was 12, we moved to San Francisco. It had rained so little we couldn't grow enough food on our farm to live. The only help the government would give was to "relocate" us to a city. They believed Indians would become more like other Americans if they lived away from other Indians.

When we got to San Francisco, my family and I were shocked! We had never had indoor toilets or electricity. We were used to night sounds of crickets and coyotes, so we were frightened by the city sounds of sirens and cars. Our hotel had a box that opened up in the wall. People got into it, it closed up, and they disappeared! My brothers and sisters and I walked up the stairs instead of using that elevator so we would not disappear too.

I did not feel I belonged in the city. After many years, we finally got used to San Francisco. I graduated from high school, got married and had two daughters.

In 1969, after a group of Native Americans protested the way Indians were being treated, I realized I needed to return to our land to help the Cherokee people. My daughters and I moved to Oklahoma where I built a new house near my childhood home. I went to college and worked to improve living conditions in our area.

During those years, I was in a car accident and it took seventeen operations for me to walk again. Then they discovered I had a muscular disease. I still take medicine for this. Finally, I needed a kidney transplant. As always, my family helped. My brother gave me one of his kidneys.

At the time I was elected Chief of the Cherokee Nation, many people thought the Cherokee people would not want a woman to be chief. But before the white people came, Cherokee women were as important as men in our culture. I believe I have followed in the footsteps of Cherokee women before me and that my people are more concerned about jobs and education than about whether or not the tribe is run by a woman.

I am no longer chief, but I will continue my work. We are a modern people who need to hold on to the best of our past: our language, our ceremonies and our culture. That is the challenge of the future for all Native Americans and I am one part of that struggle.

VILMA MARTINEZ
(1943–   )

Hello, I'm Vilma Martinez. I'm an attorney in Los Angeles. I handle cases for workers who feel they have not been treated fairly. Can everyone hear me? I know I speak softly; as a matter of fact, I never shout. I believe WHAT you say is more important than how loudly you say it.

I grew up in a poor neighborhood in San Antonio, Texas. I was the oldest of five children. One day, my family was very excited because our church group was going on a picnic. At the last minute, it was canceled because Mexican Americans were not allowed to use the park. We felt very hurt and angry.

I knew that to make things better, I would have to DO something about it. I learned how to speak English and studied very hard in school.

I went on to college and after I graduated, decided to go to Columbia Law School. I applied for money to help pay for my classes. I was told that women get married and have children and do not practice law, and that the money would be wasted. I said I hadn't been working SO long and SO hard not to practice law, and I got the scholarship money!

I graduated when I was 24. I met my future husband, Stuart Singer, while we were both studying for law exams. I began working as a lawyer in New York defending workers' rights. It was nice not to hear what I had heard all through school: "You are so bright—for a Mexican." Instead, I was accepted for my work as a lawyer.

In 1968, the Mexican American Legal Defense and Educational Fund, or MALDEF, was started, and later, I became the head of it. MALDEF did many things to help Mexican Americans, including getting voting ballots printed in Spanish for those who do not speak English and winning the right for children in public schools who do not speak English to be taught in both English and Spanish.

I later left MALDEF and joined the law firm I am with today. I like practicing law and having more time to spend with my sons, Carlos and Ricardo.

I feel lucky that I've been able to help Mexican American citizens in this country. We have made great progress, but there is still much to be done so that our country can deliver on its promise of equal opportunity for all its people.

BARBARA MCCLINTOCK (1902–1992)

Have you ever wondered why the kernels on Indian corn are different colors and how they got that way? I did and, after years of research, I discovered it was caused by "jumping genes." Genes are found in the cells of all living things. All of you have genes. Your genes make you different from everyone else. They decide your hair color, your eye color, whether you're a boy or a girl, and many other things about you.

Oh, by the way, my name is Barbara McClintock and I'm a research scientist. I was born in Connecticut in 1902. My parents taught me to find my own interests, and I liked reading, ice skating and sitting alone thinking about things.

When I was in high school, I liked math and science because it was fun working on problems and finding the answers. After I graduated, I wanted to go to college, but my parents were against it because my family didn't have enough money to pay for it. So, I got a job, but I spent my nights and weekends at the library studying. Finally, my parents saw how important college was to me, and they agreed to let me go.

I enrolled in Cornell University where I studied botany. I was especially interested in studying plant cells. I was good at preparing cells for viewing under a microscope, and always paid close attention to everything I saw.

I studied the genes of maize, or "Indian corn." A lot of my time was spent planting, tending and harvesting maize. It was hard work, but I loved it. I learned a lot about the patterns on kernels of maize.

When I finished college, I couldn't find a job as a research scientist, so I continued to grow maize at Cornell. I finally ended up at Cold Spring Harbor, New York, an important research center for scientists from around the world.

I continued my work on maize, which led to my discovery of jumping genes. Jumping genes can move from one place to another inside of a cell. Before I discovered them, most scientists believed that genes did not move, and many scientists laughed at my discovery because it was so different from what was known at the time. But I knew that my findings were right and I knew someday other scientists would understand.

Many years later, my ideas were accepted and I received many important awards. I was happy to be honored, but I was happiest of all growing and studying the maize plant. "It was fun. I couldn't wait to get up in the morning!"

MARIA MITCHELL
(1818–1889)

It's going to be cold up here, but what a perfectly clear night for sweeping the skies. How many of you have ever looked at the stars through a telescope? When I was your age, I spent many nights doing just that with my father. We would climb up on the roof of our house and look at the stars for hours.

We lived on the island of Nantucket in those days. Many of our neighbors were sailors and captains from whaling ships, and the stars helped the ships find their way home. Captains came to my father to have their instruments set correctly, so they would not get lost or have a shipwreck. He taught me how to do it too. This meant doing very hard math problems, but I liked doing them.

For a while, I was a school teacher. Then I became the librarian for our town. It was the perfect job for me. When there were no questions to answer, I could read as much as I wanted.

Did you see that? [*Point into the distant sky.*] It looked like a shooting star. Tonight reminds me of a night when I was 29. My parents were having a small party, but I just wanted to go up to the telescope on the roof. I was looking in the area of the North Star when I thought I saw a small blurry spot I had never noticed before. I ran to get my father. He looked through the telescope and checked the star charts. "It's a comet!" he said, and gave me a big hug. "You have discovered a comet above the North Star."

Did you know that if you are the first person to see a comet, it is named in your honor? Because of my discovery, I received a special gold medal from the King of Denmark. It had my name, Maria (mah-RYE-ah) Mitchell, and the date, October 1, 1847, on one side. On the other, it said, "Not in vain do we watch the setting and rising of the stars."

Years later, I was asked to teach astronomy at a new college for women called Vassar. I was nervous because I had never been to college myself. But my father thought it would be fun to tell others about the stars.

On the first day of class I told my students, "I cannot expect to make you astronomers, but I do expect to make you think." I got in trouble at times. I did not like giving grades. And one night, I cut down a tree because it was blocking my view of an important comet. I continued to teach at Vassar for twenty-two years.

It's been very nice talking with you. Please excuse me now. I must get back to my work, before it gets light.

JULIA MORGAN (1872–1957)

Hello, my name is Julia Morgan. I'm an architect. I designed more than 700 buildings in my lifetime. When I was growing up, I loved math and science. While other girls were thinking about parties and dresses, I was studying. And guess what? I got better grades than my three brothers.

Most girls those days got married after high school. But not me. When I graduated, I went straight to college to study math and science. Sometimes, I was the only girl in the whole class.

While I was in college, I decided I wanted to be an architect. I thought designing a building would be very exciting, like figuring out a hard problem step by step. And once it was built, I could look at it and be proud of my work for a long, long time. So after college, I studied architecture in France.

When I came back to California, I began designing houses for my friends and neighbors. I also worked for an architect who used reinforced concrete. Reinforced concrete has steel rods that go through it to make a building stronger. No one had ever used it in California before.

In 1906, a terrible thing happened. A giant earthquake hit San Francisco and 28,000 buildings were destroyed. But the buildings designed with reinforced concrete were still standing.

Now even more people wanted my building designs because I used reinforced concrete. I built churches and schools, and my favorite school design was one in which each classroom had a door going directly outside. Until then, most schools had long hallways or staircases, but I wanted the children to be able to get outdoors and play as quickly as possible.

I never married or had children, but I loved them. Whenever I built a house, I added something special for the children: sometimes a secret closet, or a hidden stairway or a playhouse. I wanted children to have fun in the houses where they grew up.

One day, a famous publisher named William Randolph Hearst asked me to build a grand house for him. He had collected furniture and paintings from old castles far away, and he wanted a place to put them. It took 20 years to build what is now known as Hearst Castle. It has 165 rooms, many beautiful gardens and pools.

I continued to design buildings until I was 79 years old. My buildings are the gifts I leave; they will speak for me long after I am gone.

ALICE PAUL
(1885–1977)

Did you ever believe in something so much you were willing to do anything, even go to jail, to help people realize you were right? Well, I did. My name is Alice Stokes Paul and I spent my life working for equal rights for women.

I was born in 1885 in New Jersey. My family believed in equal rights for all people. When I was young, girls often were not allowed to go to college, but I did. I attended five colleges and received six degrees. I went to England to study and became friends with some English suffragists who believed all people should vote, women as well as men. I worked to help them change the laws in England.

When I came home to the United States, I was still interested in women's right to vote. At that time, women were allowed to vote in only five states. I worked to pass a law called a constitutional amendment so women could vote in our own country. I got thousands of people to come to Washington to show they believed in women's right to vote. We did special things to call attention to our message. We always wore sashes and carried banners of purple, white and gold.

Every day for over a year, we picketed the White House, carrying flags and banners. People came to help us. When it was very cold, they brought us hot bricks to stand on so we could keep warm.

Many of the picketers were arrested and put in jail. Conditions in the jail were awful. One time we held a contest to see who could find the most bugs in our dinner. One woman found fifteen! Because of this, we went on a hunger strike. After a few days, the guards held us down and forced tubes through our noses and down our throats to get food into us. It was horrible and we all got quite sick. But we did not give up.

Finally the Suffrage Amendment passed and women voted in every state. This victory was important, but I did not believe it was enough. In 1923 I wrote another amendment called the Equal Rights Amendment (ERA), which would make the government treat men and women equally. It has not passed yet, but I believe some day it will.

I lived to be 92 years old and my advice to you is this: "If you believe in something, keep working to make it happen. You will succeed if you work hard and don't give up."

ANNIE SMITH PECK
(1850–1935)

My name is Annie Smith Peck. I was born in 1850, the only daughter in my family. I loved sports, but my four older brothers seldom allowed me to join their games. So I practiced hard, hoping I would be even better at sports than they were.

All my brothers attended college, and I did too. I graduated with honors in every subject. I became a teacher and was one of the first women in the United States to become a college professor.

After seeing the Matterhorn in Switzerland, I knew I wanted to become a mountain climber. I spent the next ten years climbing smaller mountains. When I finally did climb the Matterhorn, I was instantly famous, for my ability and courage, and for the "unladylike" climbing clothes I wore.

I gave up teaching and started giving talks about my adventures. I became interested in climbing unexplored mountains. Five times, I tried, unsuccessfully, to climb Mount Huascarán (wahs-kah-RAHN) in the Andes Mountains of Peru. When I was 58 years old, I tried to climb it for the sixth time. I hired two guides and four porters to carry our equipment. I took everything from woolen face masks and fur mittens to woolen underwear and tights. My hiking boots were four sizes larger than my regular shoes to make room for heavy stockings.

We began by riding on burros for several hours before camping for the night. Then we hiked to the snow line and set up our camp. We climbed across a glacier wearing boots with nails in the bottoms to grip the ice. The next day, we almost had to turn back when the porter carrying our stove fell down into a deep crack in the ice. Luckily, we rescued him and the stove.

On the last day, we began our final climb to the top. It was hard work. We had to cut steps with an ice ax most of the way. By late afternoon, we were almost there. Later, I looked up and realized that one of the guides had climbed to the top ahead of me. I was very angry because the honor of reaching the top first should have been mine, since I was the organizer of the climb. I swallowed my anger and finally climbed up to the top.

I was world famous after climbing Huascarán. The government of Peru gave me a gold medal and named the north peak "Huascarán Cumbre Ana Peck" in my honor.

I traveled and climbed mountains all my life. I never got married and never settled down in one place. My last climb was Mount Madison in New Hampshire when I was 82 years old.

Susan LaFlesche Picotte (1865–1915)

Have you ever lived someplace where everyone was different from you? It can be lonely, can't it? That's how I felt many times during my life. I was the first American Indian woman to become a medical doctor, and I often traveled far from my home in Nebraska. I am Susan LaFlesche (lah-FLESH) Picotte (pee-COT).

I was born on the Omaha Reservation in 1865. My father was chief of the Omahas. He tried to give them an example to follow. He built us a wood frame house, became a farmer and sent my sisters and me to school to learn to read and write in English. He often questioned laws that seemed unfair to the Omahas. I stood at my father's side as he helped and advised his people. All of my life, I tried to follow his example.

After attending school in New Jersey, I returned home and became a teacher. Once I helped the reservation doctor take care of a sick woman. I started thinking about doing something to help my people stay strong and healthy. I thought maybe I could do a better job than the reservation doctor, who sometimes did not seem to care whether he helped us or not. So I decided to become a doctor and went to college and medical school.

After I finished, I became the reservation school doctor, and later, doctor for the whole reservation. I had to take care of over a thousand people. Many times I had to ride on horseback to the homes of sick people. During the winters, I thought I would freeze to death as I rode across the snow-covered prairie. After only four years, I had to retire because my health was failing.

In 1894, I married and had two sons. I started practicing medicine again. My office was in our home, and every night I put a lamp in our front window to light the way for anyone who needed my help. I also worked to improve health laws. Once I wrote in my diary that, besides doctoring, I did everything from settling arguments to naming babies. I even tried to help change laws unfair to the Omahas. It seemed as if I had become the unofficial "chief" of the Omahas.

I died in 1915 when I was only 50 years old. At my funeral, the closing prayer was offered by an Omaha in my native language.

WILMA RUDOLPH (1940–1994)

My name is Wilma Rudolph. When I was born, I weighed only four and a half pounds. My parents never dreamed I would someday be the "fastest woman on earth." I grew up with twenty-one brothers and sisters. We lived in a small house with no electricity or indoor bathroom, and my mother made our clothes out of old flour sacks.

When I was 4, I got very sick. After that, my right leg was crooked and I could not move it. A doctor said I might never walk again, but my mother did not believe him, and every week for four years, I had treatments to make my leg stronger.

At 6, I was able to walk by wearing a special metal leg brace, and by the time I was 11, my leg was better. After years of always watching from the sidelines, I went out for basketball and track. When I ran in track meets, I always came in first. But one time, I went to a meet at a college and lost every race. I knew then I had a lot to learn.

That summer, I enrolled in a track program at a college and after that, I tried out for the 1956 Summer Olympic team. I was so nervous I couldn't eat. But I made the team and, at the age of 16, won a bronze medal in the women's 400-meter relay.

I later went to college, and was the first person in my family to do so. I joined the track team and worked hard to keep up my grades.

I made the 1960 Summer Olympic team. Even though I twisted my ankle during practice, I was still able to win two gold medals. My last event was the 400-meter relay. I ran the last leg of the race. As my teammate handed me the baton, I almost dropped it. That would have cost us the race. Suddenly, all my training was put to the test. I sprinted hard, stretching to cross the finish line first. My team did win, and I became the first American woman to win three gold medals in one Olympics.

A few years later, I graduated from college and became a teacher and a track coach. I believed it was important to give something back to sports and to people, so I founded the Wilma Rudolph Foundation, which gives free training to young athletes.

I always enjoyed talking with young people about my challenges and successes. "My. . . life is an example of what a person can achieve, even if he or she comes from a family of twenty-two children and has to overcome illness and hardship."

YOSHIKO UCHIDA (1921–1992)

My parents were born in Japan, but my sister and I were born in California. We were proud to be American, but when people saw me, they usually saw only my Japanese face. Teachers had a problem pronouncing my name, Yoshiko (YOSH-ko) Uchida (Oo-CHEE-da), even when I shortened it to Yoshi.

I began writing when we got our first puppy. I wrote down everything he did. I also started writing down everything that happened to me. It was fun, and at 10, I wrote my first story, "Jimmy Chipmunk." By 12, I had written my first book.

When I was 16, I started college. Just before I graduated, there was a big war between Japan and the United States.

Suddenly, all the Japanese people in the United States were considered "enemy aliens," even those of us who were American citizens. We had done nothing wrong; we just looked like the enemy. People were rude to us and soon we were forced to leave our nice house with its flower garden and fruit trees. We had to get rid of everything we owned, even our dog.

We were taken in buses to a big racetrack with a barbed wire fence around it. My family had to live in a horse stall big enough for only one horse. It was dark and cold and smelly in there. Guards watched us all day. We had to be in our stall every night at six o'clock for roll call. We were never alone. We wanted to get out of that place, but instead we were moved to an internment camp called Topaz. There were 8,000 Japanese people there. It was very windy. Dirt and sand covered everything.

I taught second grade in that camp. When I saw my classroom for the first time, I was shocked. There was a big hole in the roof, no tables, no chairs, no books and no heat. Many children got sick.

After a while, some people were allowed to leave Topaz. I was permitted to go and finish college, and my sister left for a new job. It was sad to leave our parents in the camp, but they were happy for us. After I graduated, I became a school teacher in Philadelphia. My parents finally joined us, and we all lived together again.

When I visited Japan as an adult, I discovered its beauty. I wrote a book about the first Japanese people who lived in America. I also wrote about the internment camps so people would not allow such a horrible thing to happen again. We must always remember that freedom is the most precious thing we have.

Appendix

SAMPLE LETTER TO SCHOOL DISTRICTS

[*Body of a letter to school superintendents, curriculum directors and/or school board members introducing* Profiles of Women Past & Present *and requesting approval to schedule classroom presentations. Send in January.*]

In celebration of National Women's History Month in March, (*name of organization*) would like to provide students in your district the opportunity to meet women from history through a series of classroom "living history" presentations. For five consecutive days, volunteer presenters from (*name of organization*) will visit classrooms, in costume, portraying notable women from history. The short presentations will be provided at no cost to the school district or to individual schools.

The women to be portrayed are: (*list of women selected*).

These presentations of *Profiles of Women Past & Present* will give your students the opportunity to meet remarkable women who have overcome obstacles and reached their goals. They will discover the many important contributions women have made to our society. Girls will be provided with positive role models. Finally, all students will be introduced to the wealth of women's history often omitted from history and social science textbooks.

With your approval, we will contact the principals at all elementary and/or intermediate schools in your district to schedule the presentations. Please contact (*name and phone number of person coordinating presentations*) if you have any questions.

SAMPLE LETTER TO SCHOOL PRINCIPALS

[*Body of letter to school principals announcing* Profiles of Women Past & Present *and providing details about scheduling. Send as soon as possible after securing appropriate approval from superintendent, curriculum director and/or school board. Copies of illustrations of the five women to be portrayed, Suggested Classroom Activities, Suggested References and Announcement Flyer for teachers can be included with this letter. Send copy to superintendent, director of curriculum, and/or school board as a follow-up to the letter introducing the presentations.*]

In celebration of National Women's History Month in March, (*name of organization*) would like to provide your students the opportunity to meet women from history through a series of five-minute, classroom "living history" presentations during the week of (*dates*). For five consecutive days, we will provide volunteer presenters to visit your classrooms, in costume, portraying notable women from history. The presentations will be provided at no cost to your school and will require no extra work for your teachers. We have obtained approval from (*appropriate information*) to schedule these presentations at your school.

The women to be portrayed are: (*list of women selected*).

The presenters assigned to your school will contact you directly no later than (*date—about one month before presentations*) to introduce themselves and to determine the best time during the day for the presentations to be made. The number of classes will determine the amount of time needed at your school. Each day during the week the classroom visits are made, the presenters will check in with you or your school secretary before they begin to see if there are any special considerations for that day. Please give your teachers a schedule for the week, and let them know the presenters will wait to be acknowledged before beginning their presentations.

These presentations of *Profiles of Women Past & Present* will give your students the opportunity to meet remarkable women who have overcome obstacles and reached their goals. The students will discover the many important contributions women have made to our society. Girls will be provided with positive role models. Finally, all students will be introduced to the wealth of women's history often omitted from history/social science textbooks.

We thank you for your support of these presentations. Please contact (*name and phone number of person coordinating presentations*) if you have any questions.

SAMPLE LETTER TO CLASSROOM PRESENTERS

[Body of confirmation letter to presenters regarding contacts with their assigned school. Send after obtaining appropriate school district approval, sending letters to principals and recruiting the volunteer presenters.]

Thank you for volunteering to portray (_____ name of woman _____) at (_____ name of school _____) on (_____ date _____) as part of this year's presentations of *Profiles of Women Past & Present*.

Please follow these procedures when contacting and making the presentations at your assigned school:

1. By NO LATER than (*date referred to in letter to principals*), please contact the principal or secretary at your school to introduce yourself and to determine the best time during the day for your presentations.

   Contact: (principal's name and phone number)

2. The day of the presentations, check in with the principal or secretary when you arrive at the school to see if there are any special considerations for that day.

3. When entering each classroom, wait for the teacher to acknowledge your presence before you begin your presentation.

Thank you for making time in your busy schedule to make women's history "come alive" for the students in our community. Please contact (*name and phone number of person coordinating presentations*) if you have any questions.

SAMPLE MEDIA RELEASE

[Send 2 to 3 weeks in advance to local newspapers and/or media. The format given is correct, but the body of the release should be double spaced.]

NEWS RELEASE

FOR IMMEDIATE RELEASE

DATE: (date the release is submitted)

CONTACT: (name and phone number of *person coordinating presentations*)

(name of organization) VOLUNTEERS TO PRESENT
PROFILES OF WOMEN PAST & PRESENT AT LOCAL SCHOOLS

Members of (*name of organization*) will provide women's history presentations at local schools during the week of (*dates*) to celebrate National Women's History Month. Volunteers will visit classrooms, in costume, and portray five notable women from history. The women who will be portrayed are: (*list of five women to be portrayed*).

These presentations of *Profiles of Women Past & Present* were initiated in 1987 by the Thousand Oaks, California, Branch of the American Association of University Women (AAUW) to introduce students to the many important contributions women have made to society and to the wealth of women's history often omitted from history and social science textbooks.

SAMPLE RADIO/TELEVISION SPOTS

[Submit fifteen-second radio/television spots, along with media release, to the person in charge of public service announcements at local radio and/or television stations. Follow up with a phone call to see if the station will tape volunteers reading the spots for broadcast during Women's History Month.]

Examples:

From 1985 to 1994, I was the Principal Chief of the Cherokee Nation, the second largest Native American tribe. My people are more concerned about jobs and education than about whether or not the tribe is run by a woman. I am Wilma Mankiller.

In college, I decided I wanted to be an architect. I thought designing a building would be exciting and challenging. It took 20 years to build the Hearst Castle in San Simeon, California. I am Julia Morgan.

My interest in mountain climbing began the first time I saw the Matterhorn in Switzerland. My last climb was Mount Madison in New Hampshire when I was 82 years old. I am Annie Smith Peck.

SAMPLE ANNOUNCEMENT FLYER

Coming Soon!

Profiles of Women
Past & Present

WHAT: Classroom "visits" by five notable women in history (each approximately five minutes in length with costumes and props):

(list of women selected)

WHY: To introduce students to the many important contributions women have made to society and to the wealth of women's history often left out of history and social science textbooks

WHO: *(name of organization)*

WHEN: *(date)*

WHERE: *(name of school)*

Teachers: Here is a chance to have National Women's History Month "come alive" in your classroom without any effort on your part.

If it is not convenient for a woman to visit your classroom on a particular day, please let your principal or school secretary know.

(name and phone number of person coordinating presentations)

Suggested Classroom Activities

1. Have the students make posters or collages celebrating Women's History Month for a classroom, cafeteria or school library display.

2. Have the students bring in pictures or articles about women from newspapers or magazines for a Women's History Month bulletin board in the classroom or elsewhere.

3. Assign a biography about a woman for the students' next book report.

4. Have the students research and write their own living history monologues, either about a woman in history, or their mother, grandmother, or other significant woman in their lives.

5. Schedule a filmstrip, movie, or video, etc., during Women's History Month to introduce students to the many contributions of women to society.

6. Integrate women's history throughout the curriculum. For example, read a story by Yoshiko Uchida during English or Language Arts, include Barbara McClintock or Maria Mitchell in your science class, or run some of Wilma Rudolph's races during recess or P.E.

7. Play "What's My Line?" in the classroom with women in history as the "guests."

8. Prepare a crossword puzzle or word search for the students using the names or descriptions of contributions of women in history as clues.

9. Have students research and write brief "news" articles about women in history. Have them answer: Who, What, When, Where, Why and How? Assemble the articles into a classroom Women's History Month newspaper.

10. Have students research information about a particular woman in history. Then, have them take turns interviewing each other during a classroom "Women in the News" program.

11. Read aloud a biography of a woman during Women's History Month.

12. Duplicate the full-page illustrations found in *Profiles of Women Past & Present* for classroom use.

13. Have the students write a letter to their favorite woman at the conclusion of the classroom presentations and send it to the woman who portrayed her.

14. Play "Hangwoman" using the names of famous women in history.

15. Have students write a speech they would give to nominate a famous woman to the National Women's Hall of Fame.

Suggested Women's History References

Altman, Susan. *Extraordinary Black Americans From Colonial to Contemporary Times*. Chicago: Children's Press, 1989.

Aten, Jerry. *Women in History: Discovering America's Famous Women Through Research-Related Activities*. Carthage, IL: Good Apple, Inc., 1986.

Bataille, Gretchen M., ed. *Native American Women. A Biographical Dictionary*. New York: Garland Publishing, 1993.

Clark, Judith Freeman. *Almanac of American Women in the 20th Century*. New York: Prentice Hall, 1987.

Davis, Flora. *Moving the Mountain: The Women's Movement in America Since 1960*. New York: Simon & Schuster, 1991.

Evans, Sara M. *Born for Liberty: A History of Women in America*. New York: Free Press, 1989.

Forster, Margaret. *Significant Sisters: The Grassroots of Active Feminism, 1839–1939*. New York: Knopf, 1985.

Great Athletes. Pasadena, CA: Salem Press, 1992.

Gridley, Marion E. *American Indian Women*. New York: Hawthorn Books, 1974.

Hine, Darlene Clark, ed. *Black Women in America. An Historical Encyclopedia*. Brooklyn, NY: Carlson Publishing, Inc., 1993.

Hudson, Wade and Valerie Wilson Wesley. *Afro-bets Book of Black Heroes from A to Z*. East Orange, NJ: Just Us Books, Inc., 1988.

James, Edward T., ed. *Notable American Women 1607–1950: A Biographical Dictionary*. Cambridge, MA: Belknap Press of Harvard University Press, 1974.

Jones, Betty Millsaps. *Wonder Women of Sports*. New York: Random House, 1981.

Loeb, Catherine, Susan E. Searing and Esther F. Stineman. *Women's Studies: A Recommended Core Bibliography*. Littleton, CO: Libraries Unlimited, 1987.

Mainiero, Lina, ed. *American Women Writers: A Critical Reference Guide from Colonial Times to the Present*. New York: Frederick Ungar Publishing Co., 1982.

Metzger, Linda, ed. *Black Writers*. Detroit: Gale Research, Inc., 1989.

Nelson, Mariah Burton. *Are We Winning Yet? How Women are Changing Sports and Sports are Changing Women*. New York: Random House, 1991.

Salem, Dorothy G., ed. *African American Women: A Biographical Dictionary*. New York: Garland Publishing, 1993.

Sherr, Lynn and Jurate Kazickas. *Susan B. Anthony Slept Here. A National Guide to Women's Landmarks*. New York: Times Books, 1994.

Sicherman, Barbara and Carol Hurd Green, eds. *Notable American Women: The Modern Period*. Cambridge, MA: Belknap Press of Harvard University Press, 1980.

Smith, Jessie Carney, ed. *Notable Black American Women*. Detroit: Gale Research, Inc., 1992.

Sterling, Dorothy, ed. *We Are Your Sisters: Black Women in the Nineteenth Century*. New York: W. W. Norton, 1984.

Tauber, Cynthia M., ed. *Statistical Handbook on Women in America*. Phoenix, AZ: Oryx Press, 1991.

Telgen, Diane and Jim Kamp, eds. *Notable Hispanic American Women*. Detroit: Gale Research, Inc., 1993.

Tierney, Helen, ed. *Women's Studies Encyclopedia*. New York: Greenwood Press, 1991.

Uglow, Jennifer S. *The Continuum Dictionary of Women's Biography*. New York, Continuum, 1989.

Wandersee, Winifred D. *On the Move: American Women in the 1970s*. Boston: Twayne Publishers, 1988.

Wayne, Bennett, ed. *Women Who Dared to Be Different*. Champaign, IL: Garrard Publishing Co, 1973.

Woolum, Janet. *Outstanding American Women Athletes: Who They Are and How They Influenced Sports in America*. Phoenix, AZ: Oryx Press, 1992.

Zophy, Angela Howard, ed. *Handbook of American Women's History*. New York: Garland Publishing, 1990.

AAUW Information

The American Association of University Women (AAUW), founded in 1881, is the oldest and largest national organization working for education and equity for all women and girls. Membership is open to all graduates holding a baccalaureate or higher degree from a regionally accredited college or university. In principle and in practice, AAUW values and seeks a diverse membership. There shall be no barriers to full participation in this organization on the basis of gender, race, creed, age, sexual orientation, national origin, or disability. For information about joining AAUW, call 1-800-821-4364.

A portion of the proceeds from sales of this book will be used to fund scholarships and fellowships through the AAUW Educational Foundation. This Foundation provides funds to advance education, research, and self-development for women, and to foster equity and positive societal change.